Female Foibles

To a special cousin
Charmil

Jack Runninger

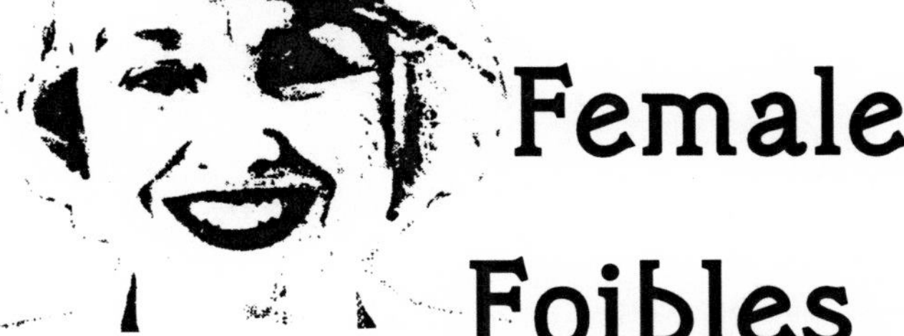

Funny Female Foibles

ISBN 978-0-9833643-6-8

cover and interior design Dekie Hicks

wheredepony press
rome georgia USA
www.wheredeponypress.com

printed in the United States of America

To my late wife Mary, and my present wife, What's Her Name, for putting up with such a sorry husband.

FOREWORD

Jack Runninger is a funny man, and he proves it when he writes. For three decades, this longtime Roman (of the Georgia variety) has been a popular humor columnist for the *Rome News-Tribune,* of which I was editor in chief for eight years.

His musings on daily life and people's antics have added a complementary dose of color and levity to the newspaper and to readers' days. His columns have earned him and the daily newspaper many state and national awards for humor writing.

In his slice-of-life columns, Jack churns out advice, observations and barbs sure to amuse.

In this book, you'll get to enjoy perhaps the best of Jack's columns on a topic on which he purports to be an expert – women. That's because Jack's family tree seems to bloom mostly female.

So that's fertile ground for Jack's comedic touch as he espouses his personal take on so many of our womanly foibles, points of view and actions.

He's smart enough to know that we gals usually come equipped with a good sense of humor and are not threatened by his holding up a mirror to help us not only laugh at ourselves, but also at the differences between men and women that human encounters expose.

Of course, the most understanding of all the women he targets has to be his lovely wife Helen Cobb Runninger, to whom Jack often refers to as What's Her Name as he writes about her and their life together.

Even as he takes aim with his sharp wit, Jack celebrates and embraces our gender differences and sparks smiles and laughter along the way. Those inclined to be defensive about his pokes and jabs about women should be savvy enough to read between the lines and recognize that in many instances he's also making fun of his own male perspective.

That's because while his columns are humorous commentary on life – and in this case on women, Jack is nothing if not a gentleman. I have been a fan of both the writer and the man for some time.

We are fortunate that Jack keeps lifting our spirits with his good-natured scrutiny.

—Charlotte Atkins
Editor-in-Chief
Rome News-Tribune, 2003-2011

PREFACE

"It is a husband's duty to periodically point out to their wives their faults, in order to give them an opportunity to improve." Thus saith some sage—I think it was Art Buchwald.

Over the past 30 years, these words have been an inspirational guide to me, and prompted me to adopt a crusade of writing columns for my local Rome (GA) *News-Tribune*. This book is a compilation of some of these columns. In them, I have generously given of my advice on how wives (specifically my own) can become better persons. Not only wives, but all females.

I have been in excellent position to observe feminine foibles, having spent my life under the domination of females, one mother, two wives (not concurrently), three daughters, and four granddaughters, with no male progeny. I finally have a great grandson, but he is but two years old, so of no help whatsoever in this battle.

It has been disheartening to discover that my advice has been universally greeted with laughter, rather than taken seriously.

"Thanks to you I've now seen the error of my ways, and will henceforth be a better person," was not the hoped for response I received from them. "That was hilarious!" was instead the comment I received. I have discovered that there are two reasons women thought the columns were funny rather than instructive.

1. They found my stupidity in not understanding the perfectly "normal" things they do to be laughable.
2. In addition, I discovered that the female species almost universally has a great sense of humor and often found humor in recognizing some of their own often unexplainable foibles or quirks. For example:

"Your column about your wife's quirks was VERY funny," emailed one lady. "I recognized myself in most of the quirks. Thank you for making me laugh at myself!

So I've given up on my curmudgeonly advice being taken seriously. But since some of the columns have received state and national Humor Column awards, you may instead get a few chuckles.

Other Books By Jack Runninger

Fixin' Stupid, co-author
You'll Do Great, If You Communicate
Junior Samples Jokebook
Going to Paris? Pack a Lunch
Favorite Jokes of Mountain Folks in Boogar Hollow

Funny Female Foibles

Adapting to What's Her Name's Quirks

May 2011

You'll note that these columns I've written are in chronological order. Except for these first two about wifely quirks, which were published recently. The reason I start with them is that they sort of set the tone for the whole book, and give my reasons for having written them. The reason I refer to my wife as What's Her Name (WHN) is that when we first married three years ago, she informed me that if I put her name in the paper, she would pound knots upon my head. Thus, obedient husband that I am, I have never called her by name in any of my columns. (Her name is Helen, by the way.)

MRS. DONOVAN WAS WALKING down O'Connell Street in Dublin when she met up with Father Flaherty.

"Top o' the mornin' to ye," said the Father. "Aren't ye Mrs. Donovan, and didn't I marry ye and yer hoosband two years ago?"

"Aye, that ye did, Father."

"And be there any wee little ones yet?"

"No, not yet, Father,"

"Well now, I'm going to Rome next week, and I'll light a candle for ye and yer hoosband."

Six years later they met again.

"Well now, Mrs. Donovan, how are ye these days, and do you have any wee ones yet."

"Oh, yes, Father! Two sets of twins, and four singles."

"That's wonderful! And how is your hoosband doing?"

"'E's gone to Rome to blow out yer freakin' candle!"

AS A PUBLIC SERVICE in these columns I have been attempting to give advice, based on my experience, to help widowers make the decision as to whether they should remarry. Thank God, having more children, as in the above story, is one of the things What's Her Name and I did not have to consider in making this decision. But what are some of the differences and faults to which I've had to adapt ?

"Don't criticize your wife's faults," some wise sage once said. "If she didn't have them, she'd have found her a better husband."

My problem is that WHN's chief fault is that she doesn't really have many faults. In fact last month for three days she was the perfect wife. (That would be the three days she had laryngitis.) What she has instead of faults that have taken getting used to, are what I've termed "quirks". For example:

SHE NEVER "LOSES" ANYTHING. "It's not lost. Everything has to be somewhere," is her philosophy. Her cell phone is one of the main culprits. Fortunately, I can call her from my phone, and she can track down the ringing noise to find it. This system, however, does not work with misplaced glasses, car keys, etc. I've unsuccessfully attempted to convince her that the only surefire system to keep from losing her glasses is one optometrist Dr. Fred Vassiere advocated many years ago:

"I want you to wear your glasses," he advised his female patients, "like you wear your pants. Put them on in the morning when you get up, and don't take them off until you go to bed at night!"

She recently even lost our cordless phone. We searched the house high and low, and never did find it. Until about three weeks later I found it when I donned a sweater, and discovered the phone in its pocket. I hate it when something turns out to be my fault!

COFFEE TABLE BOOKS. She somehow has an affinity to purchase every coffee table book she meets to give it a home. However, I guess the problem is perhaps not that we have too many of these decorative, but rarely looked at, books, but instead that we're short 842 coffee tables on which to place them.

SHE ALSO HAS NEVER MET a drinking glass she didn't like. She came home from an estate sale with three more sets of glasses, which we cannot find room for in the kitchen cabinets. "I just can't resist pretty things," she explained. (Probably the reason she married me.)

CLEANLINESS! She even cleans the house before the cleaning ladies come so that they won't have to clean a dirty house!

MULTI TASKING: Last week I found her seated in her chair, with a book in one hand, a magazine in the other, plus watching TV. Reminds me of question I got in an email from a nutty friend. "Women brag about multi-tasking. Why then can't they make love and have a headache at the same time?"

ANOTHER OF WHN'S QUIRKS is her seeming inability to realize that chairside tables are meant to hold a TV guide, the TV remote, liquid refreshments, the book I am currently reading, a pad and pen on which I can capture an erudite thought before it escapes me, etc.

She mistakenly instead thinks such tables are meant to display decorative bric-a-brac, framed photos, plant life, etc., leaving no room for the essentials I mentioned in the above paragraph.

In order to be fair, just to make certain that I was right, I took a survey of 50 people asking whether they agreed with me on this point. The results were overwhelming, 48 in favor and only 2 opposed. Coincidentally, all 48 were of the male gender, the other two were female.

POOR COMMUNICATION: WHN just doesn't do a good job of communicating verbally with her spouse. Part of the reason may be the fact that said spouse has a lousy sense of hearing, but the main cause is that her voice is so soft and accent so Southern.

"We need to see about getting a preshuh washuh," she said recently." After seven repetitions, I finally figured that what she was saying was a "pressure washer." She obviously got short changed in her Savannah education, since no one ever taught her there is an "R" in the alphabet.

A typical conversation around our house is the one we had yesterday. "It sounded like you just said 'These are good with electricity'. What are the these that are good with electricity?"

"'No, no!' she replied. 'What I said was that this cheese is good with the triscuits.

"You can always communicate by writing," you may say. Sadly, this does not work either. She seems to have an inability to read my admittedly lousy hand writing. I walked in the kitchen recently and found her sniffing the milk I had just purchased.

"Because of your note," she said when I asked her

why she was doing this. "Right there it says, 'Take milk back.'"

"No, no!" I replied. "It says 'Take Milder book!'" (Milder referred to the author of the book which I was reminding myself with the note to take someplace.)

LATELY IT SEEMS I HAVE TO WRITE such notes to myself to jog my memory. This, however, is not a perfect solution because: (a) I usually forget to later look at these reminder notes, or b) Even if I do, by the time I look at said notes, I can't read my handwriting, or (c) By the time I've taken the note pad and pen from my pocket, I've forgotten what gem it was that I was going to jot down.

(To be continued)

More on What's Her Name's Quirks

July 2011

I am a devotee of the KISS principle. (Keep It Short, Stupid). Thus in Part1 I ran out of space before I ran out of quirk material. Hence, this is Part 2.

RECENTLY WHAT'S HER NAME told me the following story, which she thought funnier than I did:

"If I should die first," said the husband to his wife, "I want you to immediately sell all my belongings."

"Why?" she asked.

"Because if you remarry, I don't want some other idiot using my stuff."

"What makes you think," she said, "that I would marry another idiot?"

You may remember, if you were paying attention, that the recent column I wrote was in regard all of WHN's quirks that I have had to adapt to for the sake of peace and harmony. Treating me with such disrespect by telling such unfunny jokes like this, is another such quirk. Also on the list:

AMONG THE TREASURES I NOW have at my humble abode is a large framed document, about the service of one Joe Brady during World War II. Plus a large box full of the pictures, memorabilia, etc. of his entire life. Who is Joe Brady?" you may ask. "Perchance a famous

Naval hero? Or a close and dear friend of WHN's?"

Wrong both times. Joe Brady is WHN's 2nd cousin. "Why, then, do we have this framed document and box of everything about his life?" I asked her.

"Well when he died, he had no wife or children to pass such memorabilia to," she replied. "Nobody else would take it, and I just thought that someone should keep it as a remembrance of him.

Such thoughtfulness is one of her quirks that makes it awfully hard for me to enjoy my old age crotchetiness, like I used to! It also takes up a whole lot of space we need for other things.

OUR SUN PORCH, ON WHICH I like to sit and read and watch the birds in the backyard, I had rechristened "The Forest Primeval." I sometimes feel that I need a machete to hack my way through all the foliage WHN has installed on the road to my chair.

It has also gradually transitioned into what I now call the "Trees and Toys Room." As she gradually purchases more and more toys for the infrequent times our great grandchildren visit, they seem to have found a permanent home underfoot in the Forest Primeval.

ANOTHER OF HER QUIRKS is that she won't realize that I am older and wiser than is she, and won't listen to what I have to say.

"Let's go out for lunch," she said Memorial Day morning.

"Not a good idea," I remonstrated. "This being a holiday, all the restaurants will be crowded and hard to get in." But finally I agreed, mainly in order to prove I was right and demonstrate my superior wisdom and foresight.

Sure enough, when we got there, the restaurant was "crowded" by the presence of two other couples. If she had only listened to me and agreed not to go, it could have saved me a whole lot of humiliation.

ALL OF MY LIFE I HAD figured that the number of pillows on a bed was determined by the number of its occupants. Two people—two pillows, etc. I discover that WHN evidently does not agree with this philosophy. Our bed has but two occupants, even when relatives come to visit, but yesterday I counted eleven pillows on it!

(It occurs to me an even worse corollary is that between the two of us, we have but two mouths with which to consume liquids, and 648 glasses with which to do so.)

It seems that pillows to her mind are not to lay one's head upon, as I had thought, but instead articles of decoration. If we did not discard nine of the eleven at bedtime, there would be no room on the bed to lay one's body.

They are not only on beds.

"Come in the living room and look," she excitedly called to me recently, after returning from shopping. I couldn't imagine what would cause such excitement, and rushed into the room to see. "Aren't those two pillows I purchased for the couch gorgeous?! Do you notice how beautifully the colors blend with the other colors in the room?"

She's asking a question like this of a slob who doesn't even notice that there ARE new pillows on the couch, let alone how their colors blend with everything?!

ANOTHER QUIRK IS ONE, like other of her quirks, that she seems to share with all womankind, namely carrying all her earthly belongings in her purse. Which becomes so crowded she never can find what she's looking for within its borders. She even found an overripe banana in it recently!!

"It appears to me you have everything except the kitchen sink in your pocketbook," I once told her when we arrived in Atlanta for some show.

"I wish I did have the kitchen sink in there," said she. When I inquired why, she said, "Because that's where I left the tickets." (For the sake of truth and honesty in journalism, I must admit this is not true. But it could have happened!)

WHN ALSO HAS A QUIRKY concept about the use of drawers. I have come to the conclusion that over the course of her life, she never owned a waste basket, so instead used her furniture drawers in which to discard trash. I have not been allowed to look through any of these drawers, but a few treasures have come to light, such as a thank you note she received from someone she had had to dinner 35 years ago, a newspaper photo of a goose riding in the front seat of a car also from the same era, and the 1970 title for an automobile that has been deceased for at least 30 years.

DESPITE BEING MARRIED to someone with so many quirks, I am almost perfectly normal myself. However, I must admit that I do have one quirk, that being that I have a big mouth. Things would undoubtedly be less stressful around the house if I would just keep my big mouth shut and not write about these things.

At least I'm not as bad as a guy I heard about recently. As he sat in the living room with his wife one evening, he said, "I love you!"

"Is that you or the beer you're drinking saying that to me?" she asked.

"Neither one," he unwisely replied. "It's me talking to the beer."

She Didn't Particularly Like the Story I Told

April 1983

The lady didn't like what I wrote. Some females are just difficult to please. Fortunately there are not many as bad as the lady in the following anecdote:

"Would you like to go to a movie?" the hosts asked a house guest who did not appear to be having a good time.

"No," she replied. "I once went to one and didn't like it."

"Would you like to play tennis?"

"Nope, I tried it once and didn't like it."

"Would you like to go swimming?"

"I tried it once and didn't like it."

"Well then, what do you want to do?"

"I'll just sit here and wait for my son to come pick me up."

"An only child, I presume," said the host.

THERE'S A LADY OPTOMETRIST at the University of California Medical Center who does not look on me with kindly benevolence. She has never met me personally; otherwise I'm certain she would be impressed with my extreme personal charm.

The reason for her lack of enthusiasm for me is a joke I told in an editorial I wrote for an optometric journal. I was attempting to make the point that everyone has good qualities, if you'll but search for them.

I thought the story made the point and was right

funny—she thought it was chauvinistic and evidently didn't see an overwhelming amount of hilarity in it.

The story was the old one about the twelve year old boy who was sent to dancing class by his parents, much against his will.

To make matters worse, he was assigned the least desirable girl in the class as his dancing partner. She was sarcastic, loud mouthed, homely, and outweighed him by a good 60 pounds. She also was a lousy dancer and had an unfortunate tendency to spend a good percentage of the time tromping on her dancing partner's feet.

"You must also learn the social graces," said the teacher to the boys in the class. "I want each of you to compliment your partner when you finish dancing."

"Whatever can I find to compliment about this girl?" asked the lad of himself as he again winced from having his toes trod upon for the sixteenth time.

But finally came an inspiration, and at the completion of the dance, he gallantly said to her, "You sweat less than any fat girl I ever danced with!"

AFTER THIS APPEARED in print, I soon received the following "fan letter" from the aforementioned lady:

"I assume you are unaware of the presence of women practicing optometry. In your recent Editor's View column, the perspiring obese dancer neither amused nor instructed me.

"Your predecessor managed to compose columns without resorting to humor at the expense of women; surely you can do the same."

IT SEEMS TO ME that too many folks nowadays, male as well as female, have lost their sense of humor, and react to a kidding as a put-down. I didn't intend for the story to be antagonistic to womankind. As I said to the lady in my letter of apology to her:

"The story was not meant to be sexist nor to offend. With one wife, three daughters, two granddaughters, (no male progeny—even the household cat is female) I could not afford to be a male chauvinist even if I was so inclined."

WHEN I WAS A MERE lad and became upset one day at being teased by a school mate, my father gave me a sage bit of advice I've always remembered:

"You should take kidding as a compliment rather than getting upset about it. People kid only folks they like! Haven't you noticed that if you don't like someone, you ignore and stay away from him, rather than kidding him?"

I enjoy teasing the female members of the species. But honestly I don't mean it to be belittling. It's really because I like womenfolk. They're better looking, softer, and usually sweeter than men. And I enjoy being kidded in return. All of us would be healthier and happier if we learned to laugh at ourselves and not take ourselves too seriously.

IT TAKES A MIXTURE OF GUTS and stupidity (mostly the latter) to address the subject of women's lib in print. Nevertheless, I feel constrained to make some observations after being accused of being a male chauvinist.

First, I agree that it is unfair that so many English terms are masculine when they are meant to include both sexes. Some of the battle between the sexes could be solved by the addition of a few new words to the English language.

One has already been accomplished—the abbreviation

"Ms." to replace "Miss," or "Mrs." in the salutation of a letter. "Mr." includes both married and unmarried men, so it makes sense to have a comparable "Ms." for married and unmarried ladies. It sure makes letter writing easier when I don't know if the lady I'm addressing is a "Miss" or a "Mrs."

I propose further that lexicographers could add three more new words to the English language:

"Se"—singular pronoun meaning either he or she.

"Hem"—singular pronoun meaning either him or her.

"Hes"—singular pronoun meaning either his or hers.

The plural words, "they," "them," and "their" include both sexes, so why shouldn't we have similar pronouns that would pertain to either male or female?

It's awkward to say, for example, "He or she should watch his or her step," instead of just using masculine pronouns to pertain to both sexes. How much simpler to change it to "SE should watch HES step." It would simplify writing while giving proper recognition to our female brethren.

(Whoops, brethren in a masculine term also. I guess I could say "brethren and sistern" but that sounds like a place to store water.)

But there are other words it appears to me should be left alone. For example, I confess I just can't get used to "chairperson" in place of "chairman."

And I'm really not ready to start calling the round iron lid in the middle of the street a "personhole cover."

A Rose By Any Other Name

June 1984

A continuing effort to see things from the female perspective.

RECENTLY THERE WAS an article in the paper about a lady who felt it was unfair for her newborn child to have only her husband's last name.

Evidently the father agreed (or got tired of arguing). So they gave the child the last name from both parents.

I think the lady is correct about the injustice of children carrying only the father's last name. But if her idea catches on, we're in BIG trouble.

Let's say Adam Camp marries Eve Gates. They name their son Abel Camp-Gates. Later, Abel marries Esther McWilliams-McDougald. Their child becomes Matthew Camp-Gates-McWilliams-McDougald.

A couple more generations and you could have a kid with a name like William Camp-Gates-McWilliams-McDougald-Byars-Fryer-Rickman-Slickman-Gray-Dickinson-Webster-Stein-Sweitzer-Barnum-Hortman-Wilcox-Allen-Dodd-Hanks-Fambro-Hubbard-Griffin-Yancey-Evans-Woodruff-Jennings-Mulrennan-Stevens-Melton-Read-Shaw-Trueblood. (What a disreputable group to be named after!)

Perhaps a better solution would be to combine

both parents' names for the offspring's first name. For example, Ferdinand and Eliza Smith could name their child Ferdiliza Smith.

THERE SEEMS TO BE a lot of interest in tracing family names. It always seemed to me the same problem applies here.

By the time you go back five generations, the guy with your family name is responsible for only 1/32 of your bloodline.

My father, after his retirement, became interested in tracing the family tree. From him I learned some things I'd just as soon not known.

The first of our tribe in America was Jacob Reiner. He was a German Hessian mercenary soldier fighting for the English during the Revolutionary War.

After the war, he decided to stay in America and settled on a farm in western Pennsylvania. Since there was a lot of ill feeling against the Hessian soldiers, he decided to "Americanize" his name by changing it to Reininger.

His descendants' time during the 19th century was spent chiefly in tilling the soil on the family farm, and trying to decide how to spell their name. Family records show spellings of Reininger, Runniger, Runinger, and finally, Runninger, during that period.

Other people seem to trace their ancestry back to war heroes, historic figures, noblemen, etc. I sort of lost interest in the whole thing when all I could find in my ancestry were people who chose a peculiar name and then never could learn how to spell it.

ABOUT FIFTEEN YEARS AGO, my father, brother, and I arranged to meet at the old family homeplace just outside Franklin, PA.

Having lived in the South for 20 years, I envisioned something a little like Tara. Big plantation house, stately columns, etc. Instead it was so rundown and small, the present tenants had moved into a mobile home and were keeping pigs in the old family "mansion."

Then came the clincher. My father's sister, my Aunt Grace, turned to my father the evening of our first day together and said: "Jack reminds me exactly of Uncle Sam."

Uncle Sam was Sam Black, my grandmother's younger brother. I had seen pictures of him and he wasn't a bad looking gent, so I was rather flattered.

Then I made the mistake of asking her to tell me more of Uncle Sam. I wish I hadn't.

Uncle Sam was the one who absconded with company funds, and leaped off a bridge when found out.

As I re-read the above, it sounds as if I'm ashamed of my ancestry. I'm not. They weren't rich or famous, but they were evidently good, hard working folks (except for Uncle Sam). It's just that it's more acceptable to kid about your ancestry than to brag about it.

"A rose by any other name would smell as sweet," is an oft-quoted Shakespearean phrase. The implication is, of course, that the label has nothing to do with the qualities of a thing, or person.

I DON'T KNOW THAT I agree with this. It seems to me that people may often live to their names.

Doesn't it seem likely that the same person would behave differently if his name were Reginald VanSnootingham than if it were Hiram Snagglewart? (If true, I'd rather have Hiram than Reginald as a friend.)

Fortunately if you have a name you don't like or that

is too cumbersome, you can always go to court and have it changed.

I've heard a rumor that this is what one local citizen did.

"I hate my name and want to change it," he told Judge Walther.

"What is your name?" asked the judge.

"Burgett Wojeickowinweskobramovitch."

"I don't blame you for wanting it changed. What new name have you chosen?"

"Joseph Wojeickowinweskobramovitch."

The British Ain't All That Dignified

November 1984

As I continue to show that I do love women despite any criticisms of their foibles. Maggie Thatcher was a person I admired perhaps as much or more than any other person.

"THE BRITISH PEOPLE are inclined to procrastinate," said a Britisher during a symposium I attended a few years ago.

"For example the Englishman with a hole in his shoe will tend to 'make do' and put off having it fixed."

"Oh, but you must have a hole in your shoe!" protested Professor Harry Freeman, another English member of the panel. "Otherwise, you couldn't put your foot in it!"

It really isn't all that funny. But the combination of the dry wit and the English accent made me crack up.

The British have a reputation as being rather humorless. But I think they have a wonderful dry wit.

Winston Churchill is another good example.

"If you were my husband, I'd give you a dose of poison," a lady member of Parliament said to him during a heated debate.

"Madam, if you were my wife, I'd gladly take the poison," was his perfect reply.

THE BRITISH ALSO HAVE a reputation as being

very staid, reserved, and dignified. I discovered on a trip to England a few years ago that this image is also not justified.

In London, my Athens, Tennessee buddy, Bill Sullins, and I were supposed to attend a day of lectures commemorating the 400th anniversary of the Worshipful Order of Spectacle Makers. (Honest! That's the real name of that Guild.)

Then we discovered that on that very day, there was to be the pomp, pageantry, and ceremony of the Queen installing Maggie Thatcher as the new prime minister.

Since the Worshipful Order of Spectacle Makers had existed without us for 400 years, we figured they could perhaps survive without us one more day.

So we skipped their meeting and instead watched the marvelous pageantry of the Queen's procession from Buckingham Palace to the House of Parliament.

Staying at our hotel was a member of the House of Commons from Aberdeen, Scotland. From him, we learned how we could tell the guards at Parliament we had a message for him, and thus get in the building.

BILL SULLINS CAN CHARM the horns off a billy goat. After we got into the reception area, he struck up a conversation with a lady from the Solicitor's office.

"If a member of the House of Lords is called Lord So and So, what do you call a member of the House of Commons?" was the question that was bothering us and which he asked her.

In response to his charm, or possibly to get rid of us and our dumb questions, she finally asked us, "Would you like for me to get passes for the Visitor's Gallery to see Mrs. Thatcher give her inaugural speech?"

Bill and I, of course, leapt at the chance to observe such an historic occasion.

But what I didn't realize was the passes she obtained for us were diplomatic passes.

"Ah yes, I see you chaps are diplomats from the States," the guard said as he admitted us.

"Duh!" I replied Snerdishly, impressing the guard, I'm certain, with the suavity and dignity of the U. S. Diplomatic Corps.

There were only two seats left in the gallery, not together. I took the one between two elderly British ladies, which until then had been occupied by their packages, purses, and umbrellas.

"You have separated my sistah and me!" one of them hissed accusingly in my ear.

Ever the gentleman, I arose, bowed, and allowed them to move next to each other as I reseated myself at the side of, rather than between, them.

IT WAS A FASCINATING EXPERIENCE to hear Maggie Thatcher's first speech as Prime Minister. It was also a surprising experience.

I expected the English statesmen to be models of decorum and politeness.

Boy, was I ever wrong!

Members in the first rows were propping their feet on top of the table in the center that held all the sacred memorabilia, etc.

And whenever the opposition disagreed with something Maggie said, they'd interrupt her either with derogatory sounds, or start arguing with her in the midst of her speech.

Far from the picture of the dignified Englishmen I

expected!

But I'll tell you something. That lady is sharp! She came out first in all the verbal exchanges with her detractors.

Come to think of it, we never did find out what you're supposed to call a member of the House of Commons.

But it's obviously not "Your Dignity."

Hell Hath No Fury Like That Of A Woman Scorned

February 1985

The late Nick Powers and I wrote a book, Favorite Jokes of Mountain Folks in Boogar Hollow, *an analysis of Southern redneck humor. A lot of this humor is based on their frankness and honesty. They never worry about being diplomatic in talking about their wives. One example, "My wife's an angel," said one. "You're lucky," replied the other. "Mine is still living."*

In the following treatise, I am amazed at how Southern Baptists, like rednecks, are so much braver than I, in their dealings with women.

"IF I SHOULD DIE FIRST, would you marry again?" she asked.

"Gee, I'd never thought about it," he replied. "I really don't think so. Possibly after six or eight years I might. But only because I'd be so lonely without you."

"If you did, would you let her live in my house?" she persisted, as wives will at times.

"Of course not!" he responded. "Unless, of course, we couldn't find any other place to live."

"Well, would you let her have my mink coat?"

"I really hadn't thought about it. If I should remarry and if she didn't have a mink, I guess I might possibly let her use it."

"Would you let her use my golf clubs?"

"No, she couldn't do that. She's left handed."

IT APPEARS TO ME that some Southern Baptist gentlemen had done messed things up with their wives just about as bad as the above gentleman.

According to a UPI news item last week:

"The Southern Baptist Convention, without debating the substance of the issue, went or record Thursday in opposition to ordination of women to the ministry.

"Women's subservient role," it said, "is because of their responsibility for bringing sin into the world.

"Less than half the registered delegates voted on the resolution." (I sure don't blame the other 50% for being too chicken to vote.)

Misery loves company. We Methodists screw up often enough—it's kind of nice to see another denomination get into trouble.

"Hell hath no fury like that of a woman scorned," according to William Shakespeare or Will Rogers or some such philosopher.

IN MY VAST EXPERIENCE living with womankind (one wife, three daughters, two granddaughters, and four optometric assistants) I've discovered (among other things):

» The best way to make a female-type person want to do something is to tell her she can't.
» Any mention of their having a subservient role is like waving a red flag in front of a bull.
» They don't even like to be blamed for leaving the bathroom light on, let alone all the sins of the world.

Thus, I don't believe I'd care to have been a male

Southern Baptist delegate as he returned home from the convention. I suspect many of them were forced to suffer through some cold meals and cold nights.

IT ALSO OCCURS TO ME that Baptists must have less need for money than we Methodists.

I've heard that women control about 75% of the money in this country. And there's another version of the Golden Rule, namely:

"Them that has the gold, make the rules."

If I were raising money to support a church, I don't believe I'd alienate the folks who control the purse strings.

It's Mostly Henry Ford's Fault

November 1986

A stressful experience!

I READ SOMEPLACE that divorce is much more prevalent in the 20th century than it was in the 19th century.

That sounds plausible. The automobile hadn't been invented yet in the 19th century.

Teaching a wife to drive a mule rather than a car just had to cause a whole lot less argument.

In 1946 I was fresh out of the Navy, and back in college in Memphis with a newly-acquired wife.

The GI Bill was paying my school expenses. My bride had a job that paid the rent and put food on the table. Between the two, I was being supported adequately, if not luxuriously.

In fact, by 1947 we were able to dig up 200 bucks out of the budget to buy a 1937 Chrysler Royal with Free Wheeling. Since the brakes didn't work half the time, it was REALLY Free Wheeling.

Since Miss Mary was supporting me, I figured I'd reciprocate by teaching her to drive.

Fortunately the marriage was a good and strong one. It had to be to survive the driver's training experience.

"Don't watch me. It makes me nervous," she'd say.

So I'd close my eyes, which was the best way to put up with her driving anyway.

"What did I do wrong?" she'd ask as the car would jump, stall, and end up over the curb.

"How can I tell if you won't let me watch you?" I'd reply, a trace of hysteria creeping into my voice.

"Don't yell at me!" she'd say. Which I never understood since, like all husbands, I was always very calm and quiet in my suggestions.

ONE SATURDAY NIGHT she was driving us to a friend's house. The route took us through the main intersection at Crump Station at the precise time 25,000 people were arriving for a football game.

She panicked and stalled the car right smack in the middle of the intersection, completely blocking traffic in all four directions.

The cacophony of horns and "gentle" words of advice from her husband created still more panic, and she couldn't get the car started again.

Without saying a word she got out of the driver's seat, and climbed into the back seat. Thus it was left to me to take over the controls and absorb the dirty looks and shouting from impatient motorists, as I unsuccessfully attempted to start the flooded engine.

HER UNFORTUNATE TENDENCY to "desert the ship" in times of crisis (she wouldn't have made a very good Ship's Captain) continued after we and the Chrysler first moved to Rome.

"Mary asked me to call and tell you the car is stalled in the middle of the South Broad Bridge," a friend phoned. "She got a ride home and wants you to go get the car."

Two weeks later the brakes gave way and I again

received a call at the office requesting that I come rescue the car which was perched halfway over a ten foot embankment.

Being a fairly lucid person, I realized a turning point had arrived in my life, and I was either going to have to either:

(A) Get rid of the car, or
(B) Get rid of the wife.

Some quick mental arithmetic convinced me that solution (A) would be a heckuva lot cheaper than (B). So I traded the car.

ANOTHER PROBLEM CONCERNING autos that causes marital discord is back seat driving.

I read somewhere of the man who cured his wife of this fault. He had the steering wheel loosened and an attachment added to the steering column that allowed him to steer with his knees.

The next day they were doing 65 mph on a crowded freeway. His wife was doing her customary job of telling him how to drive.

"If you don't like the way I drive, then YOU drive!" he screamed, as he removed the steering wheel from the column and handed it to her.

She reportedly fainted.

WHENEVER ANYTHING GOES WRONG, why do wives always assume their husbands are at fault?

Recently I read about a pilot who landed his light plane on a freeway when his engine conked out.

He went over to a car that had pulled off the road out of his way, intending to ask for help.

The woman sitting next to the driver shouted, "We'll get out of the way if you'll show us where to go! My husband is the only driver I know who could start out on a freeway and end up in the middle of an airport!"

Even Siamese Twins Could Do It, or, How to Put One's Life Together

July 1993

Another Boogar Hollow story:

I ain't seed Cousin Abe in a long time 'til yestiddy, 'n I asks him whar he's bin.

"I got married," he sez.

"That's good," I sez.

"Well, hit ain't TOO good," he sez. "She's awful ugly."

"That's too bad," I sez.

"Well, hit ain't too bad," he sez. "She's got an awful lot of money."

"That's good," I sez.

"Well, hit ain't TOO good," he sez. "She's awful stingy."

"That's too bad," I sez.

"Well, it ain't too bad," he sez. "She did buy me a house."

"That's good," I sez.

"Well, it ain't TOO good," he sez. "Hit's done burned down."

"That's too bad," I sez.

"Well, hit weren't TOO bad," he sez. "She were in it."

Obviously the wives of the original Siamese twins also had it good and bad. A fascinating story!

RECENTLY I READ an article about research being done with twins. It described the togetherness and bonding they have.

But if twins have togetherness and bonding, what about the original Siamese twins? Their story is one of the most fascinating I've ever heard. In addition, I think it contains a great moral.

Although I had heard of them, I didn't really know much about them until I met Kester Sink on a trip to Kenya. It turned out that his first wife was the granddaughter of one of the Siamese twins, and his home in Mount Airy, N.C. is the original home built by one of the twins 150 years ago. (We later visited him there, and saw some of the history of the twins. Mount Airy, you'll recall, is also famed as the home of Andy Griffith and the model for the town of Mayberry on his TV show.) Kester is the one who told me the enthralling story of Eng and Chang Bunker.

They were born in Siam in 1811 of Chinese parents, so actually they were Chinese twins rather than Siamese twins. A Scot trader discovered them when they were 13 years old. He saw swimming in the river what he thought was a strange animal—four legs, four arms and two heads swimming in perfect coordination.

IMAGINE HIS SURPRISE when he discovered they were actually two separate people connected at the chest by a 6-inch long band of cartilage. They had learned to turn their bodies sufficiently so that they faced forward, rather than facing each other. Thus, with their inner arms around each other, they were able to move in a forward direction.

The trader arranged for the two boys, whose names were Eng and Chang, to come to the United States when they were 18 years old. For the next few years, they toured cities throughout the country.

They were not just sideshow freaks. Both were highly intelligent and their performance consisted of acrobatics and lecturing.

During their travels, they decided to purchase land in the Mount Airy area and live there when they weren't traveling. There they met and married sisters, daughters of a local farmer.

They lived together in the same house at first. Then Eng and Chang each built his own house, a few miles from each other. They would spend three days with one wife, and then three days with the other.

The arrangement evidently worked quite well, because Eng and his wife ended up with 11 children. Chang and his wife were not as prolific, only having 10 children. There is little known about how they could have such active sex lives while always accompanied by a third person, but it certainly boggles the imagination!

THE OTHER INTERESTING (and heart rending) part of the story is about their later years. When they were about 60 years old, Chang had a stroke. Eng was still in good health, but he, of course, had to stay in bed with his ill brother.

Chang recovered sufficiently so that they could still move about some, although with great difficulty. But he became depressed and took to drinking heavily. He was often raging drunk and quarrelsome, which made things pretty tough for Eng.

During the course of their lives they had consulted many surgeons as to the advisability of being separated. Each one had felt it would be too dangerous, since it was not known whether they shared any organs inside their connecting band.

You can well imagine Eng's panic as Chang's health deteriorated. So he got a local surgeon to agree to separate them as soon as Chang died.

One night when they were 63, Eng awoke and realized that Chang was dead. He summoned his wife and the surgeon was notified. By the time he arrived, Eng, even though he had been in good health, was also dead. The autopsy revealed that Eng had probably died of sheer fright.

THE LONGER I live, the more I'm convinced that one of the secrets to a satisfying life is to adapt to things as they are, rather than agonizing they are not as we wish they were. Eng and Chang are perfect examples.

I cannot imagine the horror of going through life attached this way. Yet they made the best of it, and lived a fruitful and productive life. It's a good story to remember when you think life isn't treating you right.

Griping at Grouches

December 1993

Women probably have a good excuse for being grouchy around men at times. It could be because of men's grouchy behavior. A retired general was in the hospital. Always in a bad mood, he kept interfering in everything the nurses did. "Today, we have to take your temperature rectally," said one of the nurses. Grumbling all the while, the general finally agreed as she turned him over onto his stomach, and raised his gown. Other personnel kept coming in to look, so he finally growled, "Haven't you ever seen temperature taken rectally before?"

"Yes," said one of them. "But never before with a daffodil inserted where the thermometer should be."

"YOUR PENANCE IS SEVEN YEARS of silence," the novitiate in the monastery was told.

At the end of this seven-year period, he was called before the monks and informed that he had the privilege of speaking two words before entering another seven-year period of silence.

"Food's bad!" were the two words he spoke. After the second seven-year period of silence, he was again allowed two words.

"Bed's hard!" he said, and was again required to enter a seven-year period of silence. At the end of this third seven years, he was again called before the monks and allowed two more words.

"I quit!" he said.

"You might as well," replied one of the monks. "All you've done is gripe and complain ever since you've been here!"

DEALING WITH COMPLAINERS and/or grouches has always been difficult for me, as I suspect it is for you also. However, over the years I've gradually begun to adapt better as I've learned to understand them, and how best to react.

Grouches often don't realize they're grouchy.

My friend Ralph Drew was born and raised in Wales and has a delightful British accent. He also has a great understanding of people and what makes them tick.

A couple of years ago, we were having breakfast together at the Hilton Hotel Coffee Shop in New York City.

"I've been coming to this meeting for 10 years," I told Ralph. "Every year I've had the same waitress we have today. In that 10 years, never once have I seen her smile. She has a perpetual scowl."

"My friend here has just been telling me what a delightful smile you have," said Ralph in his charming accent and manner to the waitress when she returned to take our order.

I couldn't decide whether first to kill him and then slide under the table, or vice versa. Before I could do either, the waitress turned to me and I awaited the verbal lashing I was about to receive. Instead she flashed a beautiful smile at me, and said fervently, "Why, thank you!"

THE POINT BEING, of course, she had no idea she

never smiled and came across as a grouch.

There may be a good reason the person is grouchy.

A friend told me of a department store clerk who was decidedly unfriendly and unhelpful. He was extremely irritated with her. Until he discovered that her back was killing her so that he could understand the reason behind her behavior.

Don't let complainer/grouches influence your behavior.

I ONCE READ of a New Yorker who stopped at the same news stand every morning to buy a newspaper.

"Good morning!" he would say enthusiastically to the news vendor. "Isn't it a lovely morning?"

"Grrrr," was the grouchy vendor's invariable response.

"Why are you always so friendly to that news vendor, when he is always so unfriendly to you?" his companion asked him one day.

"Because I'm not going to let a grouch like that determine how I act," he responded.

FINALLY, I'VE DISCOVERED it's best not to argue with people who don't behave as they should. Be like the truck driver who was being harassed in a truck stop by three motorcycle hoods. One of them poured water down his back, another took his steak away from him and began to eat it, and the third one stole his hat from off his head.

The truck driver didn't argue or complain. He calmly got up, paid his check, and left the restaurant.

"He sure wasn't much of a man," said one of the hoods to the waitress. "He was scared to stand up to us."

"He's not much of a truck driver, either," she said. "He just ran over three motorcycles when he left the parking lot."

Being Married This Long is 50/50 Proposition

August 1995

Actually, it's not a 50/50 proposition! As some sage has said, "The secret of a happy marriage for a man is when he's wrong in an argument with his wife, admit it. And when he's right, just shut up."

"I'VE BEEN PRETTY GOOD TO YOU, haven't I? I told you when we got married 50 years ago that I'd carry you over all the rough places in life," said the husband.

"That's right," said the wife. "And you haven't missed a single one of them, either."

My better half undoubtedly understands and appreciates this story, since we just celebrated our 50th. Among other nice things our daughters did to recognize the occasion, they surprised us by providing a copy of our wedding picture to the *Rome News-Tribune*.

The reason they sent in our wedding picture rather than a current photo is that we didn't have a current photo. But I think they've stumbled onto something. Everyone keeps telling us what a great idea it was to have the wedding photo in the paper instead of a picture of a couple of old wrinkled folks.

So if you're going to have a photo in the paper for a 50th anniversary, you might ought to send in a wedding picture to prove to people that you were a lot better looking back 50 years ago.

Some despicable people like John Pinson sent cards of condolences to my better half. But nicer people kept congratulating us on achieving our 50th. I really can't figure out why it's considered an event deserving of congratulations. It's not that great an accomplishment; all you have to do is live long enough, and avoid a divorce.

LIKE THE COUPLE WHO couldn't get a divorce because neither one of them would agree to take the children. Or another example:

"What do you want for Christmas?" asked the husband of his mate.

"A divorce!" she replied.

I wasn't planning on spending that much money!" he countered.

I first met her when she was sophomore in high school. Although we lived in the same town, our paths never crossed since she attended West Aurora (Illinois) High School and, living on the other side of the river, I went to East Aurora.

It was on a double date. She was a comely lass with a lovely face, good figure, and hair so blonde it was almost white. I'm afraid I didn't pay much attention to my date during the evening.

She was obviously also smitten by my charm and good looks, because she asked me for a date soon thereafter. I had best hasten to explain that it was a high school sorority party where females were supposed to do the asking, or else I might never make it to a 51st anniversary.

Six years later, I was able to convince her that I should be the one to carry her over the aforementioned rough places in life.

Since I did not know her during her formative years, I had no idea of how she had spent them. However, I was soon to discover that she had not devoted a great deal of that time to honing her cooking skills.

She was a little bit like the bride who prepared her first meal for her new husband. As she placed the food in front of him, she apologized. "I've only learned to cook two things, meat loaf and apple pie."

"Which one is this?" he inquired after taking the first bite.

BUT I'LL HAVE TO ADMIT that she gradually became an excellent cook. Which was quite surprising for one who has demonstrated a distressing tendency to prefer the golf course and bridge table to cooking and keeping house.

"Where do you want to go on vacation?" comedian Henny Youngman says he asked his wife.

"Someplace I've never been before," she replied.

"How about the kitchen?" he answered.

I would never, never be so insensitive or chauvinistic as to tell a story like that on my wife. Nor the following one, either:

"I've been a good wife," sobbed the wife to the marriage counselor. "But he keeps gambling away all our money!"

"Some good wife!" exclaimed her mate. "Two months ago I pawned the kitchen stove to get money to bet on a horse race. She still hasn't noticed that it's gone!"

And I have more sense than the husband who on his 50th anniversary kidded, "We've had some really good years together. Let's see, there was 1948, 1954, 1958, and 1961 wasn't too bad."

Husbands Losers in Battle of Sexes

February 1996

"You're wearing your wedding ring on the wrong finger!"
"I know. I married the wrong man!"

"IT SAYS HERE THAT I'M A DYNAMIC leader of men, and irresistible to women," said the man as he read the card from one of those coin scales that dispense weight and fortune.

"It has your weight wrong, too," replied his wife after glancing at the card.

Why is it that we husbands get absolutely no respect from our wives? We are so perfect in almost everything we do, yet seldom get credit from our mates! They eternally and forever remember the few mistakes we make, but seldom recall the good things we do.

"How did your wife react when she discovered what you did?" one errant husband was asked.

"She got historical," he replied.

"You mean 'hysterical,' not 'historical.'"

"No, I mean 'historical.' She brought up everything I had ever done wrong since we first got married."

I'm certain many of the unwarranted accusations I have suffered through the years are typical of what many other husbands have endured.

"You forgot to bring the camera," said my child

bride (she fusses at me when I refer to her as my "aging bride") as we watched our granddaughter Beth play in her final age 10-and-under basketball game.

DO YOU NOTICE THE SUBTLE SHIFT in blame? It seems to me that she forgot the camera just as much as I did, but somehow I was the one who did the forgetting. Other example of my purported transgressions:

- "You've tracked dirt in the house again. Why can't you remember to take off your shoes like I do?"
- "I don't see how you splash water all over the bathroom when you shower. It doesn't happen to me."
- "Why does the roll of toilet paper always end up unrolled to the floor after you use it?"

But recently I had a triumph, which although miniscule, has given me ammunition in this continuing battle of the sexes:

"It's the strangest thing," said my bride as she unloaded the washing machine. "Whenever I wash clothes, my shirts always turn inside out, but yours don't."

She will live to regret this admission. Whenever I am now admonished for any misbehavior, I reply, "Yes, but at least my shirts don't turn inside out in the washing machine like yours do!" One small step for husbandkind.

AS THE MAN ON THE APPROPRIATE side of the street shouted during Lady Godiva's naked sidesaddle ride through the streets of Coventry, "Hooray for our side!'

I Should Have Known Better Than to Mess Around with Dear Abby

June 1996

Another lady I admire is Abigail Van Buren (Dear Abby), even though that's not her real name.

IT WASN'T THE FIRST time I ever screwed up. And it undoubtedly won't be the last. But I should have known better

What happened was that a recent Dear Abby column in the *Rome News-Tribune* contained a letter that discussed the difficulty of remembering names. It reminded me of an occurrence I'd read about, so I wrote Abby to tell her about it. She published it in her column. Part of my letter read:

"I remember a true story from many years ago that illustrates the danger of pretending to know who someone is.

"A lady couldn't remember the name of someone she ran into on the street one day. As she racked her brain, the other lady finally mentioned something about her brother.

"'Oh yes . . . your dear brother . . . what is he doing these days?' she asked, figuring this might give her a clue to the lady's identity.

"'Oh, he's still the President of the United States,' she

replied. (She was Calvin Coolidge's sister.)"

A COUPLE OF WEEKS later another letter appeared in Dear Abby. It was from someone in Texas, and in essence said,

"It would be a little difficult for a sister of President Coolidge to discuss his being president of the United States. His only sister died almost 30 years before he was ever elected."

It proved that I had succumbed to the "if it appears in print, it must be true" blunder. I learned once again to take the truth of what I read with a grain of salt.

I wrote to apologize to Abby. She published that letter also, as a preliminary to other letters she'd received attributing the same story to other famous persons.

Abigail Van Buren must be the most widely read author in the world. After my letter appeared in her column, I heard from old friends and former Romans from far and wide.

"When I saw your name signed to a letter in Dear Abby, I was afraid it was concerning some kinky sex problem," an old college friend wrote from Michigan. "I was relieved to see that such was not the case."

PROBABLY MY ONLY claim to fame is that I have now been published in Dear Abby four times. Some friends say this indicates she may be becoming senile.

The first time was some 10 to 15 years ago. The letter I wrote was in regard to chain letters. In retrospect, it was really kind of a stupid letter. Fortunately for me, Abby did not sign my name to it, but instead signed it "J.R. in Rome, Ga."

"Probably many people in Rome wondered just who is the local person who would write such an idiotic letter,"

I wrote in a *Rome News-Tribune* column at the time. "But I was pretty well covered because it is obvious that I am not the only idiot in Rome with those initials.

"Jack Robbins, Julian Reese, and John Read are three more examples that immediately spring to mind." The second time happened about four or five years ago. One of the letters in Abby's column came from a new bride who complained about going to a hotel on her honeymoon, and discovering the bridal suite wasn't furnished yet. I couldn't resist sending Abby a story this reminded me of, and she again published it.

"I know of a similar experience," I wrote her. A local bride told a friend that she and her husband on their honeymoon at a new hotel discovered that their bridal suite didn't yet have a bed or a couch.

"What was your reaction?" asked the friend.

"I was floored!" she replied.

Elders Aren't Hostile to Jests

November 1996

"If'n I get married, will I live longer?" I asks ole Doc Adams. (again from Boogar Hollow book).

"I don't know," sez Doc. "But it sure will seem longer!"

THE BURGLAR WAS casing a house to make certain no one was home before he entered it. As he peered through a window, he heard a voice say, "Jesus sees you!"

Startled, he looked around but saw no one. He figured he must be hearing voices, until he noticed a parrot in the back of the room, who again said, "Jesus sees you!"

"There seems to be no one home except for that nutty parrot," he said to himself, "so it should be safe to rob." He climbed through the window and came face to face with a large, ferocious, snarling dog.

"Sic him, Jesus," said the parrot to the dog.

This story was told to me by a bus driver character at a recent elder hostel we attended at Armstrong Atlantic State University in Savannah.

"What is an elder hostel?" you may ask. An elder hostel is a little bit like a kindergarten for a senior citizen's second childhood. Just as back when you were five or six years old, you go to class, and you go on field trips, and you play silly games.

One of the games the first night (it did have a purpose—getting to know the other attendees better) posed kind of an interesting problem. We divided into groups and were asked to answer the question, "If you were shipwrecked on an uninhabited island, what five people would you like to have with you?"

FORTY YEARS AGO, all of the males' lists would have undoubtedly started with "Marilyn Monroe." (A number of years ago, actress Madeline Carroll was asked what male she would select to be stranded with on a desert island. "An obstetrician!" was her very practical answer.)

Either all the husbands were afraid of their wives' wrath, or at this more advanced age they decided their answers should be more on the practical rather than hormonal side. Thus Marilyn received nary a vote from the husbands present. The most frequent answers from both males and females were:

Robinson Crusoe and Friday. (To have someone who has been through this before and knows what to do.) This suggestion prompted a terrible story from the group:

"Two fleas got together on Robinson Crusoe, and had such a good time they decided to meet again on Friday."

Daniel Boone. (To hunt and supply food.)

Julia Child. (To cook the food.)

Dr. DeBakey. (To have a physician to treat physical ills. Another elder suggested Dr. Kevorkian in case all else failed.)

Marconi. (To figure a way to signal for help.)

Noah. (To build an ark in which to escape.)

Bill Clinton. (If the U.S. President was missing, the CIA would have to mount an intensive search.)

Moses. (To part the waters in order to escape.)

I SNEAKED A LOOK at Mistress Mary's paper, because I was certain that she had placed me as her first choice as to whom she wanted with her on the island. I was quite shocked and hurt to note that not only was I not her first choice, I wasn't anywhere on her list!

I guess she related to the lady in the story that late humorist Leo Aikman used to tell about the elderly couple sitting and rocking in their living room one night.

"We've been married 50 years," said the husband to himself. "She's cooked for me and kept house and never complained, and I've never taken her anyplace, or done anything for her, or thanked her for all she does for me. It's time for me to tell her I appreciate her." So he turned to his wife, who was a little hard of hearing, and said:

"I'm proud of you!"

Without looking up or missing a stroke on her knitting, she replied, "I'm tired of you, too!"

OK, Fellas, This Time the Joke's on You

December 1996

"What are you doing today?" asked the retiree's wife.
"Nothin'," he says.
"That's what you did all day yesterday."
"I didn't get finished."
Much as I hate to admit it, men are not perfect.

THERE ARE A FEW troublemakers in Rome, Georgia. They keep asking my bride, "How do you let your husband get away with making disparaging remarks about you in the paper?"

I have repeatedly assured her that I was only joshing, but a few more remarks from the grandstands and she could become rebellious. Recognizing the old saying, "If momma ain't happy, ain't nobody happy," I hasten to try to rectify the situation by presenting a few items that make males rather than females the butt of the joke. I don't find them to be particularly funny, but female members of our species seem to enjoy them. The first example:

"Stand back!" shouted a male bystander as he elbowed aside a lady who was bending over a pedestrian who had passed out on the sidewalk. "I'll take care of this. I've had first aid training!"

"Ok," replied the elbowed-aside lady. "And when

you get to the part about calling a doctor, I'll be right here."

Another contribution I received consisted of riddles that slander the male sex. But I shall include them herewith anyway, since the purpose of this column is to make points with the weaker (??) sex.

Q. What is the difference between government bonds and men?

A. Bonds mature.

Q. What do men and beer bottles have in common?

A. They are both empty from the neck up.

Q. How many men does it take to change a roll of toilet paper?

A. We don't know. No man has ever changed a roll of toilet paper.

THAT LAST ONE IS particularly unfair. I can remember at least two occasions when I did so. And besides, women often just don't understand efficiency.

Why go to all the bother of changing the roll, and then having it in an awkward position when it's needed? How much easier to have it in one's hands to unroll, rather than having to be a contortionist to bend around and back to reach the paper holder! And then, when you pull to try to tear off the amount you need, either (a) the roller is too loose and you pull half the roll off the roller and onto the floor, or (b) the roller is too tight and refuses to give up any paper other than a small scrap, woefully inadequate for its purpose.

Even though men are superior at efficiency, I will admit that women are better at neatness. I can relate to the gentleman who went to the bathroom in the middle of the night. When he came back to the bedroom, he found that his wife had made up his bed.

Q. What's a man's idea of helping with the housework?

A. Lifting his legs so you can vacuum.

Q. What's the difference between a man and E.T.?

A. E.T. phoned home.

IN THE FURTHER INTEREST of getting on the good side of female readers, I shall refrain from including the following anecdote I recently read:

"I'd like to marry your daughter," said the young swain to his beloved's father.

"Have you seen her mother?" asked the father.

"Yes, but I'd like to marry her anyway."

YOU WILL NOTE that this column is comparatively short. There are just so few things to write about when discussing male shortcomings.

Never Too Old to Give Learning a Quick Shot

August 1997

Another Boogar Hollow story: Cousin Mary Ann went to the sheriff last week to tell him her husband wuz a' missin'. The sheriff sez, "You'll have to give me a description of him."

"Well," she sez. "He's little 'n skinny 'n wrinkled 'n bald, 'n wears glasses and false teeth. Come to think of it, most of him was missin' afore he was."

Losing your good looks as you get older doesn't mean you can't improve your mind.

"LINE ME UP five shot glasses of Bushmill's," said the Irishman to the bartender. When the bartender finished pouring them, the Irishman tossed them off quickly, one right after the other.

"I've never seen anyone consume five shots that fast!" said the bartender in amazement.

"You have to drink them quickly when you've got what I've got," replied the Irishman.

"And what is it you've got?"

"About 90 cents total."

My aging, but still beautiful and charming bride, our 11-year-old granddaughter, and I attended an elder hostel at Amicalola Falls State Park the first week in August. The purpose of elderhostels is for old folks to learn new things. The Irish story was told me by the program coordinator, so I guess it qualifies as learning a new thing.

But I did learn some other things as well. As a public service, I shall hereby relate these fascinating bits of information, so that you may become as learned as I am.

I LEARNED THAT Amicalola (near Dahlonega) is the highest waterfall east of the Mississippi River, more than 700 feet high. We hiked to its foot, and it was an impressive sight.

We were told by some lyin' ranger that snakes are our friends. He may have sold some of the more gullible attendees on this, but not me! I still feel like Lewis Grizzard's friend who said, "If it ain't got no shoulders, fergit it!"

Granddaughter Beth is young, sweet, and impressionable, so he was able to convince her that snakes really are friendly. She and the other 12 grandkids present all were coerced into holding a big rat snake, but most of us grandparents were unconvinced and kept our distance.

I learned (the hard way) that running into a log while traversing rapids in a canoe will upset the canoe and its occupants. Also that it is much easier and quicker to upset a canoe than it is to get the water out of it and turn it back upright. Not a terribly important lesson to learn, since I do not foresee ever having to use this bit of information again.

I learned that wishes do not always come true. One morning two Indians lectured to us about the culture and history of the Indians of the Southeast. They were dressed in all the Indian regalia along with painted faces.

They decided they would go canoeing down the river with us that afternoon, still dressed in their garb and war paint typical of the early 1800s, even though neither one of them had ever been in a canoe before.

My fervent wish was that there would be a fisherman who had consumed a six-pack somewhere along the shore of the river. I would have loved to have seen his expression when he saw two Indians in war paint come around the bend of the river in a canoe.

After covering a slippery, narrow, rainy four miles at the beginning of the Appalachian Trail, I soon learned that I have absolutely no desire to complete the other 2,096 miles.

I learned that the gold mines in Dahlonega have played out, but they have discovered another gold mine in all the tourists. Going through an old mine reminded me of my favorite song title, "She Got the Gold Mine, I Got the Shaft."

I learned that there is a bookstore in Dahlonega that specializes in old books. I was able to find one of my boyhood heroes, Robert Benchley. Three of his comments I remember to this day:

1. After getting caught in a rainstorm, he said, "I can't wait to get out of these wet clothes and into a dry martini."
2. He had been completely ignored by the doorman at a swank hotel during his entire stay. Until he checked out and was leaving. The doorman then held out his hand for a tip, and said, "You're not going to forget me, are you?" To which Benchley, while grasping and fervently shaking the doorman's hand, said, "Of course not! I'll

write every day."

3. He told of a friend who was afraid to have a fourth child because he had heard that every fourth baby was Chinese.

AND AS WE LEFT, I did learn one more Irish joke from the coordinator:

"Tell me about the penguins you have here in Atlanta," said the Irish tourist to the bartender after ordering a drink.

"There ain't any penguins in Atlanta," replied the bartender.

"Sure and you'd better make it a double then," said the Irishman. "I believe I just ran over a nun!"

Don't Pick on Dogs . . . Just Bark About Wives

November 1997

Including a discussion of why they always answer a question with another question.

"DO I TURN left at the next intersection?" I asked the lady who shares my home, as we were driving to some destination that escapes me at the moment.

"Do you mean to tell me that you have lived in Rome, Georgia for almost 50 years and still don't know how to get to (a destination that escapes me)?" said she.

"Look, I was not requesting a discussion of my admittedly poor sense of direction," I unwisely replied. "The only response I was looking for was whether or not to turn at the intersection, which we have now passed, so it's too late to find out anyway!"

Somehow we finally got to where we were going, but not via wifely directions, since she wasn't speaking to me by that time.

Anyway, it got me to thinking: Why do wives always answer a question with a question rather than an answer?

I have a friend who has the same problem. Recently he asked his wife: "Why do you always answer my question with another question?"

"Why do you ask?" she replied.

"WHY ARE YOU WRITING about wives, again?" you may ask. There are three reasons:

1. I've discovered it is safer to write about the shortcomings of wives rather than those of dogs. I caught all kinds of hell from dog lovers about my recent dog column. This doesn't happen when I write about spouses.

Which leads me to the conclusion that people evidently like their dogs better than they do their mates.

2. "When are you going to write about wives again?" and "What I enjoy most is when you write about wife problems" are the most common reactions I get from males. I've finally figured out why. They don't have the guts to talk back to their wives, so they vicariously enjoy seeing me do it, thereby getting in the dog house.

Speaking of dog houses, all husbands have been in the dog house at one time or another. But Jerry Hubbard is the first one I've ever heard of who had the dog house come to him. He was driving behind a pickup truck filled with junk, when a dog house came loose from the truck, flew through the air, and smashed his car's front end.

3. Columnist Art Buchwald points out that it is the duty of all husband to periodically point out the deficiencies of their

wives in order to give them an opportunity to improve.

SOMEONE HAS POINTED OUT that Adam and Eve were probably the only couple to have a perfect marriage. That's because he couldn't brag about his mother's cooking, and she couldn't complain about all the other men she could have married.

Other husbands, braver than I, have pointed out other imperfections of wives:

» "We've been married 50 years," said one contributor to the *Atlanta Constitution's* Vent column. "My wife is a good old gal, comfortable as an old shoe. But like an old shoe, every part of her is worn out except for the tongue."
» "I always introduce my wife as my 'first wife.' It keeps her on her toes.
» "The reason wives take their knitting with them, is so they'll have something to think about while they are talking."
» "Marriage isn't a word; it's a sentence."
» "My wife's cooking is so bad, the flies got together and mended the screen door."
» "The doctor, when he examined her, told me 'I don't like the looks of your wife.' I told him I didn't either, but she was good to the kids."
» Comedian Alan King provides a couple of good answers to use when in an argument with your wife. When she says, "I'm noth-

ing but a cook and a maid around here," you can say, "That's not true! If you were the cook and maid, you'd have been fired a long time ago!"

» And when she says, "My mother warned me I shouldn't marry you!", the best reply, according to King is, "That's the only thing your mother and I have ever agreed on!"

» "I got a new car for my wife," said one man. "Gee, I wish I could make a trade like that!" replied the other.

I HAVE TO QUIT writing now, because it's time to leave to go out for the evening. "Are you ready to go?" I just asked the lady of the house.

"Would I have my coat on if I wasn't?" was her reply.

What's Really Needed Is Pill to Cure Viagra's Popularity

July 1998

Uncle Rube's ole lady sez to him, "I'm ashamed of the way we live . . . my maw pays the rent . . . Aunt Martha buys all our clothes . . .'n my sister sends us the money fer food."

"You SHOULD be ashamed," sez Uncle Rube. "You got two uncles what don't send us a dime."

We also ought to be ashamed the PhD received less credit than the mother of 16.

IT WAS OUR FIRST get-together at the elder hostel. In order to get to know each other better, all the attendees were asked to stand and tell a little about themselves.

Among the females present were a well-educated psychiatrist and prominent educator. Did they receive applause after describing what they had accomplished? Not on your sweet bippie!

The woman who did receive applause was the one who announced that she had 16 children. Which got me to wondering again if the world had gone crazy.

Why would having 16 kids be an applaudable act? The skills necessary to accomplish this certainly aren't difficult to learn, nor painful to perform. In addition:

"One of the best things people can do for their descendants would be to sharply limit them," according to a man named Olin Miller. (Who he is I have no idea, but with the dangers of population explosion, I certainly subscribe to his statement.)

NOW COMES ANOTHER symptom of this insanity. The Clinton administration recently announced it will provide Viagra at no charge to Medicaid patients! And they still won't cover birth control pills!?

It appears to me this is backwards. We need to provide folks with a pill that will help control the population growth rather than one that can stimulate it.

In addition, I find that I resent my tax dollars being spent in this manner. Even if all the recipients were like a friend (who shall be nameless) who was having his Viagra prescription filled by a young lady pharmacist.

"While I'm here, you might as well give me a two year supply," he told her.

"How many is that?" she asked suspiciously, obviously wondering if they had a sufficient stock to grant his request.

"About six," he replied.

Besides, a recent newspaper story reveals that Viagra can be a dangerous drug. The story told of a man who was suffering extreme wrath and threats from his wife. It seems she counted his Viagra pills, and there were two he could not account for that had not involved her participation.

PERHAPS IT WOULD have been better if, rather than Viagra, Pfizer had instead developed Memoraga, a pill to restore memory function to us senior citizens. Its need is well illustrated by the following example:

A 20-year-old lady married an 80-year-old man. She figured the stress of the wedding night might be harmful to him, so she reserved two hotel rooms for the night.

She figured he could rest better after the stress of making love if he had his own room.

The old gentleman had been taking Viagra and performed quite admirably in bed. When they finished, the bride sent him next door to his own room to rest.

As she dropped off to sleep an hour later, there came a knock at the door. It was the bridegroom who, to her surprise, proceeded to make love with her again. Exhausted, she sent him back to his room again. Another hour passed, and again came a knock at her door.

"Are you back again?" she remonstrated unbelievingly.

"Oh?" confusedly responded the groom. "I've been here before?"

The Shortcomings of Wives

September 1998

"Don't be sad," said the husband, on his deathbed, to his wife. "We've had 27 pretty good years of marriage."

"That's not the right number," she replied. "We've been married 58 years."

"I know!"

Things don't always go perfectly in marriage. As in:

SHE DID IT AGAIN.

We were driving to Kennesaw State University to see granddaughter Jennifer Watson receive her MBA degree.

"Do I need to get in the right turn lane or go straight?" I asked my navigator (who doubles as my wife) as we approached an intersection.

Now if I had been driving with a male companion and asked this same question, he would have quickly solved the problem with a straightforward one word answer, either "Right" or "Straight."

Such is not the case with wives. Instead, what I heard was, "If you had paid attention and listened to me when I gave you directions, you would have known that . . ."

Fortunately I correctly guessed the way to go, as soon as I realized the directions I needed would not be forthcoming in time.

This episode helps prove three shortcomings of wives:

1. It is impossible for wives to give a succinct answer to questions from their mates. They either, as I've noted previously, respond by asking a question in return, or else precede their answer with a lengthy editorial comment as to why the question was probably unnecessary in the first place.
2. They have an unfortunate tendency to accuse us long-suffering husbands of not listening to them. "Why didn't you tell me we were going out tonight?" I whine from the depths of my easy chair. "I told you three weeks ago, but you never listen to anything I say," she replies.

I like the bumper sticker which says, "My wife says I never listen to her. At least that's what I think she said."

3. They also have the unfortunate habit of accusing husbands of not noticing or paying attention to them. This is not true. Just the other day I noticed something was altered about my bride's hair, and proceeded to make points by showing her that I was aware of the difference.

"You've changed your hair," I said.

"That's right," she replied, but not with the warmth I

had hoped for. "A week ago Wednesday."

At least I'm not as bad as the example we heard in Ireland, from comedian Hal Roach.

"Do ye notice anything different about me?" asked Finigan's wife.

"Ye've got a new dress?" he asked.

"That's not it."

"New hair style?"

"No."

"I give up. What is it?"

"I'm wearing a gas mask."

LORD KNOWS I'VE tried to help my bride become a better wife and a better person. For 53 years I've been pointing out her little faults and idiosyncrasies, so that she might have the opportunity to correct them.

But somehow, it ain't worked! I've even tried to help other downtrodden husbands by delineating common wifely deficiencies in these newspaper columns, but reports I receive indicate that other wives don't take them to heart any better than does mine.

I heard a legend the other day that many finally explain why wives don't treat us husbands with the respect, concern and solicitude we so richly deserve:

"I'm lonesome," complained Adam to the Lord.

"I have the perfect solution. I shall create a wife for you," answered the Lord.

"What's a wife, Lord?" asked Adam.

"She'll be the most sensitive, caring and beautiful creature I've ever created. She will know your every mood and how to make you happy. She will unquestioningly and uncomplainingly care for your every need and desire. She will be the perfect companion!"

"Sounds great, Lord!"

"But, it's going to cost you."

"How much, Lord?"

"An arm and a leg and an eye and an ear."

ADAM PONDERED FOR A LONG time and finally asked, "What can I get for just a rib?"

For Heaven's Sake, Don't Let Afterlife Be Boring

January 1999

If family all reunites in Heaven, what do you do if you've had three wives? Which would mean three mothers-in-law.

"I CAN'T MARRY George!" lamented the devout young lady to her mother. "He doesn't believe there's a hell."

"You go right ahead with your marriage," replied her momma. "Between the two of us we'll soon convince him."

I've had too many friends die lately. At each funeral service I am troubled by the fact that, like the young man in the story, I too have difficulty grasping the concept of an afterlife.

"She was always doing things for other people," said one of the preachers at Nancy Ward's funeral. "Now she's in heaven taking it easy while other people wait on her."

That may be a lovely thought, but it's lousy reasoning. Great lady that she was, Nancy was happiest when she was doing for others. She'd be miserable in heaven if that was taken away from her.

Heaven, as I understand it, is supposed to be a place where you have no problems, and everything and everybody is perfect. If so, it has to be mighty boring, which is a whole lot worse than being problem free.

Without problems, struggles and things to strive for, there wouldn't be much purpose in existing. It doesn't seem to me that God would sentence us to an existence without challenge.

Perhaps I am too practical and analytical in nature, but there are a number of other things about the usual image of heaven that give me concern:

» Reuniting with families. Picture the man who was twice widowed and thus has had three wives during his days on Earth.

  Will he be reunited with all three, along with their families? That means he'll have three mothers-in-law he's reunited with. And, if any of his wives had previous marriages, possibly even a couple of "husbands-in-law." Seems to me this is going to create, rather than eliminate, problems.

» Streets of gold. If I remember correctly, gold is a good conductor of heat. So on a sunny day, why would anyone want to walk on hot streets?

» Selection process. Taking only the United States into account, let's say there were four million deaths during the past year. Let's further assume that half of them are selected for heaven.

  There can't be but an infinitesimal difference in the "degree of goodness" between the person rated number 2,000,000 and the one rated 2,000,001. Doesn't it seem a mite unfair that the former makes it and the latter doesn't?

» Only Christians? I've heard it said by church pastors and laymen that the only route to heaven is through confessing Jesus Christ as your savior.

  I have many Jewish friends. Some of them are as sorry as I am. But some of them are right good people. Does their not believing in the divinity of Christ automatically relegate them to hell no matter how good a life they have led?

» Reward? We are taught that the reward for our being good is going to heaven when we die. But if that is our reason for doing the right thing, is it not then for selfish purposes? It would seem to me that we should do good because it's the right thing to do, not because we are seeking a reward in an afterlife.

I'VE COME TO TERMS with the whole question by realizing that the God who had the power and knowledge to create this marvelous universe certainly could have answers to these dilemmas, even though such solutions are completely beyond my powers of comprehension.

So if he (she?) has another place for me to go, and other things for me to do after I die, that's fine with me. If not, that's ok too. I'll never know the difference.

I just appreciate all he's done for me here on Earth.

A True Confession: Dancing at Age 11 Marred Him for Life

September 1999

"I just don't see how you drink this awful stuff!" the wife berated her husband about his excessive drinking as she took a sip of his whisky.

"See, you thought I'd been having a good time."

I also looked for an excuse for taking pot shots at womankind.

"I HAVE SERIOUS LEGAL problems, and want the best attorney in your firm," the man requested.

Unbeknownst to him, this "best" attorney was female in gender. So when she came into the conference room to discuss his problem, he chauvinistically assumed she was a secretary. "How about doing me a favor, honey," he said as he glanced up at her. "Go down to the coffee shop and get me a cup of coffee while I review these papers before discussing them with the attorney."

"Be glad to," she replied.

"Thanks, darlin'," he said when she returned with the coffee.

"No problem," she replied. "That cup of coffee just cost you $152. Two bucks for the coffee, and $150 for 15 minutes of billable time for my going after it."

A couple of folks have accused me of being as chauvinistic as the above character. They objected to what I recently wrote in the *Rome News-Tribune,* and also in *Optometric Management Magazine,* about some of the idiosyncrasies of womankind in general, and wives in particular.

"Your column is patently offensive and belies the profound level of institutionalized and individualized sexism with which our profession, indeed, our language and society, are imbued," wrote an optometrist from the state of Washington.

BUT JUST WHEN he had me feeling guilty over having ruined good will between the sexes, our first lady, Hillary Clinton, came to my rescue.

Hillary recently was able to explain that husband Bill was not responsible for his peccadilloes with women. According to her, his pursuit of other women is the result of childhood trauma, the battle for his affection between his mother and grandmother when he was a wee lad. So I figured if that excuse worked for the Clintons, I could also claim childhood trauma as my excuse for at times picking on members of the female sex. My excuse-providing trauma occurred as follows:

It was one of the worst experiences of my life. I was about 11 or 12 years old. Someone in our grade school got the bright idea that ballroom dancing should be part of our cultural training. At that age, as far as I was concerned, dancing, especially with girls, was only for sissies.

I can still remember the humiliation and resentment in attempting to guide my assigned partner, Louise Weiss, around the dance floor. For one thing, I think the Lord played a dirty trick on us when He (She?) made girls grow and mature faster than boys of that age.

Thus, the aforementioned Louise Weiss was a head taller than me, and a whole lot stronger, so that she was able to jerk me in any direction she wished to go.

BUT I THINK YOU (and Hillary) will agree that this episode absolves me of all past and future guilt in taking pot shots at womankind. It's obviously Louise Weiss's fault, not mine.

Sounds like a great system, doesn't it? Nowadays it seems we can justify almost any of our misdeeds by blaming them on other people, or previous bad experiences.

But, after giving it more thought, I wonder if it's so great after all. Is it possible that part of the reason the world has some many more problems these days is that most folks look for excuses, instead of taking responsibility for their own transgressions?

Futurists Believe the World Is Going to the Dogs

March 2000

"I got a dog for my wife."

"Sure wish I could make a trade like that!"

Possibly the smartest female of the 20th century was TV dog Lassie. But to get a female dog smart enough for the part, they always cast her with a male dog.

ACCORDING TO A NEWS item I read recently, some futurists predict the number of human births will slow in the 21st century. So much so that the world's population will level off after the year 2035.

But according to *The Futurist* magazine, replacing the people population explosion will be a quadrupling of "companion animals" during the century.

The problem, as I see it, is that if dogs are really as smart as some of their owners make them out to be, with their increasing numbers, they may soon take control of the world. Although it may be not because dogs are getting smarter, but instead that humans are getting dumber.

"God must have loved dogs because he gave them his name spelled backward," wrote one lady in a letter to the editor of a publication that had run an article she considered unfair to dogs.

And author H. Allen Smith reported of the dog

catering service that assured Catholic dog owners that their dogs would be provided only fish dinners on Friday.

And it's not only dogs we must worry about. It seems that other dumb animals ain't so dumb either.

According to an article in *People* magazine, a Beaver Falls, PA woman says her life was saved by her pet pig's brilliance. When she fell to the floor with a heart attack, her pet potbellied pig, LuLu, waddled out to the road, flagged down a motorist, and led him to her trailer in time to save her life.

If dogs and pigs ever get together, we may be in even greater danger.

"I BLAME MUCH OF the animals-are-smarter-than-humans movement on the old TV show Lassie," wrote *Sarasota Herald-Tribune* columnist David Grimes.

"Lassie, as you recall, was a collie with an IQ higher than Marilyn Von Savant. Unfortunately for Lassie, she was stuck with a bunch of humans who had trouble putting their shoes on the right feet, let alone dealing with the rigors of life in the wilderness.

"It was a good thing the Martin family had Lassie around because otherwise they would have all been dead five minutes into the first show. Mr. Martin, who apparently had been kicked in the head by a horse at some early stage of his life, chose his family's home site on the basis of how many abandoned mine shafts there were in the area and also on the number of mountain lions, which were thicker in those parts than med-flies in Bradenton.

"Timothy, who presumably had his umbilical chord knotted around his neck at birth, spent his childhood seeking out, and falling into, every abandoned mine shaft in the county. There was always a mountain lion in or near the mine shaft into which Timmy had fallen.

"Mrs. Martin spent the entire 20-year-run of the show in the kitchen, stirring a pot of something or other. But she was the smartest one of the bunch. Sometimes it would take her only 15 or 20 minutes to figure out that Lassie's barks meant that Timmy had fallen down yet another mine shaft and was in danger of drowning in the hysterical drool of laughing mountain lions."

PLAYING MY ANNUAL game of "Dodge The Multitudinous Dog Piles" while raking leaves in my yard (a particularly ripe accumulation I tracked into the house disclosed that I had once again lost the contest), reminded me of another example of intelligence.

Dogs obviously have enough sense to know that it's not their own yards they wish to befoul. So most neighborhood dogs seem to rush to my yard when the urge strikes. Thank God, I'll no longer be raking leaves a century from now if my yard deposits of doggy doo are going to quadruple!

Rare Book Admits Men Are Too Good to be True

July 2000

A classic book that should have won the Pulitzer Prize. Finally a lady who truly understands men.

"ONE REASON MEN are hard to live with," wrote Jean Kerr in her book *The Snake Has All the Lines,* "is that they insist on behaving as though this were an orderly, sensible universe. The other reason is that they're so good."

I was delighted to discover her book, written in 1960, at the most recent local library sale. At last, a woman who admits that it is the goodness of men that causes the problems between the sexes. Among the virtues of the male sex that she mentions:

A man remembers important things: "It really is remarkable the fund of information he keeps at his fingertips: the date of the Battle of Hastings, the name of the man who invented the printing press, and the formula for water," explains Ms. Kerr.

"So it is obviously unreasonable to expect one so weighted down with relevant data to remember a simple fact like what size shirt he takes, or what grade Gilbert is in, or even that you told him 15 times that the Bentleys were coming to dinner."

What she forgot to mention is wives' unfortunate

tendency to exaggerate. When she says she told her husband 15 times about the Bentleys, it means she may have told him possibly once. And that once was undoubtedly in the midst of her prattling trivia while his mind was occupied in deep thought on some important matter.

A man will give you an honest answer: "If you say, 'Honey, do you think this dress is too tight for me to wear?' he'll say, 'Yes,'" according to Ms. Kerr.

Come on, now. Most husbands aren't that stupid.

A man is reasonable: "Actually there is nothing wrong with a man's being reasonable," reasons Ms. Kerr, "so long as he doesn't insist on your being reasonable along with him.

"'Let's be reasonable,' he keeps saying with the same frequency that he says, 'Go ask your mother,' or 'What's for dinner?'

"The occasions on which he thinks you should be reasonable vary, but on the whole it's safe to say that it's any time your driven past your endurance and out of your mind by irresponsible and unreliable merchants, cleaning ladies, etc. When what you really need is a word of sympathy from him."

A man idealizes his wife: "This is another way of saying that he hasn't really looked at her in 14 years. To get me a housecoat, my husband will make the unthinkable sacrifice of entering Lord & Taylors and even penetrating the awesome portals of the lingerie department.

"There he selects the size that necessitates my having to take the thing back and get one four sizes larger."

A man will not meddle in what he considers his wife's affairs: "He may interfere at the office, driving secretaries to drink and premature marriage by snooping into file drawers, etc. But back home in the nest he is the very model of patience and laissez-faire," says Ms. Kerr.

"He will stare at you across the dining room table (as you simultaneously carve the lamb and feed the baby) and announce, in tones so piteous as to suggest that all his dreams have become ashes, "There's no salt in this shaker."

The late Jack Smith was a columnist for the *Los Angeles Times*. He also once described the thoughtfulness (often unappreciated) of husbands when he wrote:

"One thing I do, I put my breakfast and luncheon dishes in the washer to save her (his wife) that trouble, but I don't actually operate it. I think if you develop skill in the other person's field, it makes her feel less unique and useful. It's threatening. One of the main responsibilities of a spouse is to reinforce the other person's self esteem."

A man is more efficient than his wife: I confess that this one comes not from Ms. Kerr, but is instead my contribution to the subject. Women somehow do not seem to understand the efficiency involved in placing one's trousers, for example, on the back of a chair, rather than hanging them up in the closet. It's a great time saver in case one wishes to don them again within the next few days.

Along these same lines, most women also fail to grasp the efficiency involved in not washing the dirty dishes that have piled up in the sink, so long as there are still unused clean ones patiently waiting in the cupboard.

Another example of how much more efficient is the male of our species than the female: The typical man has six items in the bathroom (hairbrush, toothbrush, toothpaste, razor, shaving cream and deodorant). The average female has 342 items in the bathroom.

Despite the fact that I pick on wives, I will admit that when I got married, I married "Miss Right."

Only problem was that I didn't realize at the time that her first name was "Always."

English Gardens the Reason the Hatter Went Mad

September 2000

English "garthens" were not my cup of tea. But my wife, who is much more "couth" than am I, wanted to see and attend classes about them. Which gave me a great opportunity to play hooky, and wander the beautiful English countryside.

I, ALONG WITH my bride and Jo and Curt Melton, was a tourist in Merry Old England recently. We attended an elder hostel there studying English gardens (momma's idea, not mine). As you may know, elder hostels are supposed to be learning experiences for "senior citizens," the politically correct term for "old geezers."

And a learning experience it was!

I learned early on that English garden tours were not, as the English say, "my cup of tea." The first hint that I was in the wrong place came when I heard an Englishman say to his wife in a heavy English accent as he gazed at a plant that appeared none too remarkable to me, "If you put it in a nice clay pawt (pot), it would look rahther lovely, I think."

I learned that the best part of the program was the technical lectures on the Latin names for plants and how to plan formal and informal gardens. These gave me the opportunity to cut class and wander along the public paths in the beautiful English countryside in Kent and the Cotswolds.

I learned the word "garden" comes from the old English word "garthen," meaning an enclosure. I did feel a little more cultured after picking up this bit of information in the only lecture I attended.

I LEARNED ABOUT, and saw, the white cliffs of Dover on the English Channel. If you're sufficiently old, you'll remember the popular World War II song, "There'll be Bluebirds Over the White Cliffs of Dover."

"Only problem is, there are no bluebirds in England and never have been," our bus driver informed me when we discussed the song. "The only bird in England with 'blue' in its name is the 'blue-tit,' which is a type of chickadee."

Obviously the composer of the song felt that taking the liberty of placing bluebirds in England gave a more pleasant image than being ornithologically correct by naming the song "There'll Be Blue-tits Over the White Cliffs of Dover."

It was also in Dover that I heard the story of the swimmer who set a new record for swimming the English Channel. He swam it in 16 hours, but came back in only 15 minutes! His jock strap got caught in the pier when he began the swim.

I also learned that if you are going to climb to the top of the church tower in the town of Rye, also on the English Channel, it is best to first check your watch to make certain you will not be in the bell tower when the hour changes. My left ear was approximately three feet from a very large bell when it sounded the hour. My head is still reverberating.

I LEARNED THAT THE antiquity of buildings in England gives them a great deal of quaintness, beauty and charm, but can cause problems when they are adapted to modern-day living.

The hotel where we stayed in the Cotswolds was built as an English manor house just three years after Columbus discovered America. There was not space in our courtyard room to later add the indoor plumbing necessary to attract modern-day tourists. So they had to add the bathroom above the sleeping room. Rather disconcerting to have to traverse a steep set of stairs in the middle of the night to go to the john, or as they call it in England, the "loo."

I learned that the small Methodist church in the village of Wye has a custom that I feel should be adopted in the United States. The bulletin board on the front of the church stated, "Women's Pleasant Hour Every Other Thursday 10:00 to 11:00."

Two hours a month of women being pleasant is better than none at all!

Mostly I learned that I really didn't want to learn all that much about English gardens.

Women Are Perfect . . . Well, Almost Perfect

February 2001

God is the only one who could have taken a rib from a male and turned it into a loudspeaker.

A REPORTEDLY TRUE story: "The material we put in our stomachs," said a Jenny Craig dietician addressing a large audience, "is enough to have killed most of us years ago. Red meat is bad. Soft drinks erode your stomach lining. Chinese food is loaded with MSG.

"But there is one food that is the most dangerous of all. Can anyone here tell me what food it is that causes the most grief and suffering for years after eating it?"

A 75-year-old man in the front row stood up and said, "Wedding cake."

As I've said before, although I enjoy kidding the opposite sex's foibles, I really do like women—they're better looking, sweeter, softer and probably smarter than men. However, since I do have this high regard for them, I feel constrained to periodically point out to them their faults, in order that they may strive to improve.

One such fault is nagging. As one gentleman said, "My wife's an angel. At least I figure she must be because she's always 'harping' about something or other."

Wifely nagging even dates back to Biblical times.

"Mary rode Joseph's ass all the way to Bethlehem."

Talkative?

Wives also are at times too vocal and "know it all." As demonstrated by the want ad which read, "For sale: complete set of encyclopedias. No longer needed. Wife knows everything."

"MY WIFE IS TRYING to poison me," said a congregant to his rabbi in another anecdotal illustration, told to me by a Jewish friend. "Can you talk to her about it?"

The rabbi spoke with, or rather listened to, the wife for a period of three hours, and then returned to the husband.

"What's your advice?" the husband asked.

"Take the poison," replied the rabbi.

It recently occurred to me that I have been wrong in blaming only wives for these tendencies. Actually, it's not just wives; I've discovered the problem is inherent in all females.

I have four granddaughters, all of whom I love dearly. Three of them, Jennifer, Jody, and Beth Watson, nag just as badly as do wives. The fourth is only three years old, so hasn't started yet.

Our weekly family get together is for lunch after church on Sundays.

Invariably, these lovely granddaughters point out to me (nag) that my sport coat doesn't go with the tie I've chosen, or make some other critique of my attire.

I figured if they were going to be that critical, I'd give them something to complain about. So for Christmas Eve dinner, I wore a natty outfit consisting of red and green checked sport coat, orange polka-dotted shirt, bright red and yellow striped tie, gray and pink checked pants, red and green Christmas socks, and tennis shoes.

GRANTED, I PROBABLY am a little bit of an unsophisticate. I once took a *Reader's Digest* test which asked the participant which of a pair of designs was most artistic. I got three right out of 15. Just guessing should have given me a score of 50 percent, rather than the mere 20 percent I got right.

Nevertheless, this unsophistication does not seem to me good reason for the aforementioned granddaughters to badger me. Whatever happened to the good old days when grandchildren were polite, and treated their kindly old, gray-haired, apple-cheeked grandparents with respect and awe?

Poet and author Odgen Nash years ago came up with what may be the explanation for these distressing female proclivities. He attributed the problem to women wearing high-heel shoes. This, he maintained, causes their heads to tilt forward so that the blood flows into the speech centers of their brains, and away from the intelligence centers.

Perhaps this also explains an observation by a friend, who has five daughters, "I've come to the conclusion that females reach their peak at age 6."

Brains Go Idle When Women Shift into Drive

March 2002

In which I describe my wife's and my trials and tribulations in her attempt to learn how to drive "Little Car."

"I BOUGHT MY WIFE a second car," said comedian Dave Barry. "A tow truck."

A possible reason that women and automobiles often do not co-exist well is that there may be some component in automobiles that magnetically drains the blood away from female heads, thus causing their brains to become undernourished while driving.

Take my wife, for example. She is probably more intelligent than I am. (You may recognize this statement as a spineless, sniveling, cowardly attempt to hopefully shorten my stay in the doghouse for what I am about to relate.)

I figure that one of the proofs of her extreme intelligence is, of course, her choice of husband. Nevertheless, this brilliance does not seem to carry over once she enters an automobile.

We have a big car, which she drives, that we use for trips. I also recently purchased a little car for my use around town. A couple of weeks ago, Big Car had to go into the shop for a few days for repairs. Thus, it became necessary for her to learn to drive Little Car, or be stuck at home, which was a far worse alternative to her.

Thus on the way home from delivering Big Car to the garage, I supervised while she made a trial run and errand stops piloting Little Car. Quite an experience. Since the controls were in different places than in Big Car, she kept manipulating the wrong levers. Every time she attempted to shift the car into drive or park, she instead turned on the windshield washer. By the time we arrived home, I had the cleanest windshield in town.

THE NEXT DAY I had to attend a meeting in Atlanta. She had the choice of remaining in the hotel room while I was busy, or instead attempting to navigate Little Car around the city of Atlanta. She chose the latter.

When she made the 30 minute drive back to the hotel, I'm certain that Atlanta motorists were perplexed by the little car with its windshield wipers swishing away, on a bright, sunny day. She had inadvertently turned them on, and couldn't figure out how to turn them off.

I'll admit that I once backed into a car, but I was at least a little more selective than she in selecting the car to back into. Her experience was at Jekyll Island a number of years ago. We had been at a meeting, and she had dropped me off at the motel office to check out. When I climbed back in the car, she proceeded to back out of the parking space, smack into a car behind, crumpling its fender.

From the newly dented car poured two state troopers who were chauffeuring Georgia's Secretary of State.

But my bride is not the only female afflicted with "women's driver syndrome."

In his book *Oops!,* Art Linkletter tells of the woman driver who heard sirens and pulled over like a good citizen to the side of the road. Seconds later a fireman was pounding on her window. She had stopped smack in the middle of the fire station driveway—blocking the fire engine that was sounding the alarm.

PERHAPS THE CLASSIC EXAMPLE is the following:

A few years ago I wrote a column about urban legends, great stories that were told as having actually happened, but were probably untrue. One of these stories was about the man whose car battery was dead, so he asked a lady driver to give him a push to get started.

"I have an automatic transmission, so you're going to have to get up to about 30 mph before the car will start," he instructed her.

Too late he realized that she had misunderstood him. In the rear view mirror he saw her back up a half a block, begin roaring straight at him, and hit his stationary car while she was going the 30 mph he had requested.

The next day after the column was published I received a phone call from a local lady.

"I'm too embarrassed to tell you my name," she said. "But the story you told as being probably untrue actually happened to me. My husband's car was stalled, and he told me I'd have to get up to 30 mph to get him started.

"I was going the 30 mph when I hit his car. Luckily all I got out of the resultant collision was a broken arm."

I rest my case.

The Lady or the Tiger? Tigers Less Dangerous

October 2002

"Don't argue with your wife," is the first rule any young husband should learn. It just ain't worth the repercussions. And don't forget not to laugh when someone tells her jokes like: the three rings of marriage are first engagement ring, then wedding ring, and then suffer-ring.

"AFTER BEING MARRIED a few years," said author Robert Ruark, "I have finally learned the secret of understanding women. After all, if you spend a few years in a tiger's cage, you're going to know a whole lot more about tigers than you did before.

"The secret—women are vain, and sensitive to criticism."

Incidentally, Ruark was struck down in the prime of life and died at age 50. Which may help indicate that God is perhaps female, rather than male.

I couldn't help but think of Ruark's appraisal the other night. My bride of 57 years turned on Channel 2 on the TV, and then turned it back off when she found no Braves game on there.

"I guess they're not televising the game tonight," she said.

"It's on Channel 17. You mistakenly turned on Channel 2," I unwisely replied.

"No, I didn't," she maintained. "I punched in 17!"

After further argument, I finally figured it would be much healthier to blame the whole incident on a faulty TV remote that couldn't recognize the difference between 17 and 2 than it would be to further pursue the argument.

Unlike women, men readily admit any mistakes they make. It's just that we make so few of them. According to statistics, which I am making up as I go along, women make an average of 5.7 mistakes per day, while men make only 0.8.

For the benefit of those husbands who are more inexperienced, I herewith submit a few tips on things best left unsaid, lest they be construed as criticism.

- » Do not say when you return home from work, "What have you been doing all day?" Much better instead is to say, "I've always loved that old brown robe you're wearing."
- » Do not quote the following poem to her:

First God made man in the Garden of Eden
Then he said to himself
"There's something he's needin'."
After casting about for a suitable pearl
He kept messing around and created a girl.
Soft, cascading hair hung down over her shoulder,
And two dreamy eyes, just to make him grow bolder.
She was made for a man, just to make his heart sing.
Then God added a mouth, and ruined the whole thing!

Which reminds me of a recent study reported by the Washington Post, which concluded, "Women have better verbal skills than men." Which causes one to wonder how much money was wasted on that study!

- » When your wife tearfully complains, "You don't like my family!" do not respond, "Yes I do. I like your mother-in-law a whole lot better than I do mine."
- » Do not tell her that when Augusta National's Hootie Johnson was asked if he believed in clubs for women, he replied, "Only when kindness fails."
- » After telling your wife that her new dress fits like a glove, do not add that the reason is that it sticks out in five places.
- » The late Dr. C. R. Wilcox, who was president of Darlington School, was a braver man than I am. Reportedly, his wife once complained to him, "Man's work is from sun to sun. Women's work is never done." To which he replied, "Leave it to a woman to make a virtue out of an inadequacy."
- » Do not do as Rodney Dangerfield once did. When his wife asked him what was on TV, he replied, "Dust!" Incidentally he also once reported that he and his wife had discovered the secret to making their marriage work."Twice a week we go to a nice restaurant, have some good food, a little wine, and good companionship. She goes on Tuesdays and I go on Fridays."

But the main reason you shouldn't criticize your wife's faults is that if she didn't have them, she probably would have found herself a better husband.

Things on Which Men, Women Think Differently

September 2003

"Earl, why don't you ever close cupboard doors and drawers?" complained his wife.

"Why close them when I'll just have to open them again later?"

"Okay, I get your point. But can you at least do me a favor, and make an exception for your zipper?"

Males and females do not always see eye to eye.

FARMER BROWN'S BARN had just gone up in smoke, and his insurance agent was trying to explain that he couldn't collect cash for it. "Read the policy," he insisted. "All our company engages to do is provide you with another barn exactly like the one that's been destroyed."

"If that's the way your insurance works," replied the farmer, "cancel the policy on my wife!"

Husbands and wives don't always get along. The reason: Female and male thought patterns just do not operate on the same wavelength. Some of the many areas in which they differ:

Shopping. "Men hate to shop, I guarantee it," wrote Jeff Foxworthy in one of his books. "Just stop any man you can find and say, 'Would you rather spend the whole day shopping for clothes or having exploratory rectal surgery?' Most men would answer quickly, 'Now if I had the surgery, how long would I be out of work?'"

As a public service to husbands, I have found a foolproof system for not being asked to go shopping with your spouse. All you have to do is continually gripe, pout and whine during the whole process. This makes things so unpleasant your wife will never ask you to go with her again.

The problem is that sometimes there's no way of getting out of it. If all your trousers have holes in them, or even worse, have badly shrunk around the waistline, the only way to replace them is—go shopping. When this happens, I find that I usually buy the first thing I see so that I can quit shopping. Then when I get the purchase home I'm usually dissatisfied with it. I didn't say we were smart, just different.

Memory: Unfortunately, wives have much better memories than do husbands. "My wife is afflicted with total recall," was humorist S. J. Perelman's comment on this matter.

But they have an unfortunate tendency to remember only the bad stuff! A husband of 40 years can remember 119 of the 120 anniversary, Valentine's, and birthday occasions occurring over that period, and forgets only once out of the 120 times. What does she remember? All the times he did good? Nope, only the less than one percent of the time he screwed up.

"Eighteen years ago, I lost a key," wrote Bill Cosby. "Ever since, almost daily my wife tells our children, 'Your father always loses his keys.'"

Thoughtfulness: Women are generally credited with being more thoughtful than men. I'm not so sure this is true, as witnessed by the following episode:

While attending a marriage seminar on communication, the instructor declared, "It is essential that husbands and wives know the things that are important to each other. For example, can you describe your wife's favorite flower?" he asked the men.

"Yes," said one of the husbands. "I'm almost positive that it's Pillsbury's All-Purpose."

However, I must admit all husbands are not this thoughtful. Although I personally would not stoop to doing something so crass, I'm afraid there are some thoughtless husbands who will relate wife-demeaning stories such as this one:

"If I die first, I want you to promise to marry Tim," said the husband to his wife.

"But I thought you hated Tim," she replied.

"I do."

The Time Forrest Was Speechless

October 2003

I had to include this story about Kiki Petropole, a lady without equal.

THERE ARE TWO THINGS in particular I remember about my late friend Forrest Shropshire.

First, not only was he an excellent speaker, but also a superb conversationalist, with ready answers about almost everything. Except for this one time.

Many years ago he and I were in the same foursome in a two-ball golf tournament. The format was that each twosome would consist of a male and a female, with each alternating shots. His assigned partner was Kiki Petropole, and my partner and I were fortunate to have been the other two in the foursome.

In those days, Forrest was an excellent golfer, consistently shooting in the 70s. Kiki was not! Those of you who remember Kiki will recall that she was a great and funny lady. Also that, to state it gently, she was ample in girth. This made it very difficult for her to lean over sufficiently to strike the ball.

In addition, she had just started playing golf, and thus was far from proficient. She always wore a muumuu when she played, which added to the fun.

A typical hole that day consisted of Forrest hitting

a long drive right down the middle of the fairway. Kiki would top the ball and hit it about 10 feet, or far left or right into the rough. Forrest would then make a great recovery iron shot to the green. Kiki would then putt the ball 30 feet past the hole.

"What was our score?" Kiki asked Forrest at the completion of the round.

"We had a 95!" groused Forrest.

"Hmf!" replied Kiki. "I could have done that well by myself."

It was the only time I ever saw Forrest completely speechless.

The other chief memory I have of him is that whenever I ran into him, he always had a great smile and a good story.

THE ONE IN PARTICULAR I remember and often subsequently used in speeches and writings as an example of innovative intelligence:

A seedy-looking middle-aged gentleman, with a young, good-looking blonde on his arm, walked into a fancy fur salon in Atlanta one Saturday morning.

"I want to buy my girlfriend here a fur coat," he announced to the proprietor. Even though the proprietor was sure the man could not afford it, he showed them some coats anyway.

"This is the one I want," said the girlfriend pointing to a $10,000 mink.

"Then that's the one you shall have," said the seedy one as he began to write a check for amount on the Bank of Villa Rica.

"I'm sure your check is good," lied the proprietor, "but store policy prohibits us from taking a check of this amount without verifying it at the bank. And since it's Saturday, we will be unable to do this until Monday."

"No problem," replied the seedy one. "If you'll just set the check and coat aside, my girlfriend can come in on Monday to pick up the coat while you verify at the bank that the check is good." To which the proprietor agreed.

The following Monday afternoon, the seedy one again entered the fur salon.

"I don't know how you have the nerve to show up here!" stormed the proprietor. "Your girlfriend came by this morning to pick up the coat, and when we called the Bank of Villa Rica, they said you didn't even have ten dollars in your account, let alone $10,000!"

"I know," replied the seedy one. "I just came by to thank you for a lovely weekend."

Romance Proves an Old Story

February 2004

"My wife is becoming less attractive with age," a friend told me. "She no longer minds the airport body search. In fact, she now thanks them."

RECENTLY I WAS ASKED to give a talk to the First Methodist seniors group Valentine's Day luncheon on how romance relates to senior citizens. I devoted much time to study and research in order to make an accurate analysis.

It seems rather wasteful to allow only those few Methodists to benefit from the results of the knowledge I garnered. Thus, for your edification, I shall hereby generously share my conclusions with you as well.

Some of the anecdotes I relate to prove my points I have probably used in previous columns, but not in the context of illustrating the romance/senior citizen relationship. Besides, most seniors reading this, if they're like me, can't remember what happened yesterday, let alone stories told previously.

My study surprisingly revealed that there is an attribute of advancing age which may be beneficial to romantic success.

"I've been married for 55 years," a gentleman recounted to a young lady, "and the last 10 years have been the happiest of all 55."

"That's so sweet!" said the young lady. "What do you think is the reason?"

"Well, about 10 years ago, I started to lose my hearing. Ever since I haven't been able to hear most of what my wife says!"

ANOTHER EXAMPLE ALSO helps proved this theory that hearing loss can be helpful to romance: An elderly gentleman was prancing down the street with a peroxide blonde on his arm when he ran into his physician, Dr. Joel Todino.

"What are you doing?" asked the concerned Joel.

"I'm just doing what you advised me. You told me to be cheerful and get a hot momma."

"No, no!" said Joel. "What I told you was, 'Be careful. You've got a heart murmur.'"

I must admit however that my research revealed most of the other problems of senior years are not as conducive to romantic success.

First, our memories are not as good as they used to be. An elderly gentleman at a retirement home had a crush on a widow there, and one night asked her to marry him. The next morning he could not remember what her answer had been. So he finally had to phone her to find out.

"I'm ashamed to admit that my memory is so bad," he told her, "but for the life of me I can't remember what your answer was when I asked you to marry me."

"Oh, she said, "My answer was yes, yes, yes, and I meant it with all my heart." After a pause she continued, "As a matter of fact, I'm glad you phoned. I couldn't remember who it was that asked me."

ANOTHER HANDICAP TO romantic success is that we don't look as good as we used to. An example of this concerns an elderly lady in a retirement home. "That new man who just moved in is kind of cute," she told a friend. "But I can't get him to pay any attention to me."

"All you have to do to get him to notice you," replied the friend, "is to take off all your clothes and streak past his door." This seemed a good idea, so that's what she did.

"Did you see that lady who just went by the doorway?" the man asked a friend who was in the room. "Could you tell what she was wearing?"

"No," replied the friend. "But whatever it was, it sure did need ironing!"

The last handicap to senior's romance that I discovered is that our physical abilities are not as good as they used to be. An example is the story about the Widow Murphy having a date with 90-year-old Patrick O'Rourke. When she got home, her daughter asked if she'd had a good time.

"I had to slap his face six times," replied Mrs. Murphy.

"He got fresh with you, did he?" asked the daughter.

"No," said Mrs. Murphy. "I was trying to keep him awake."

Perhaps the best example of this problem is the old story about the couple who got married at the age of 88, and went on a two-week honeymoon.

"HOW WAS IT?" a friend of the bride asked her on their return.

"We had a good time," she replied.

"That's not what I meant," said the friend with a leer. "How often did you make love?"

"Almost every night," said the bride.

"Really?!" said the friend with surprise.

"Yes. Almost on Monday night, almost on Tuesday night, almost on Wednesday night . . ."

Sensitive Guys Don't Let Women Get Their Goat

March 2005

"Where did you get the black eye?"

"My wife gave it to me."

"I thought your wife was out of town."

"So did I!"

It seems to me that the honorable J. D. "Goat" Rankin is risking the same thing.

AFTER MY RECENT column relative to my bride's difficulties in learning to drive, I have received accusations from numerous members of the female persuasion about males in general, and me in particular, being insensitive clods.

To which I must respond, "Au contraire." We males are very sensitive in dealing with members of the opposite sex. For example, humorist Robert Steed once told about J. D. "Goat" Rankin, a "paradigm of husbandly sensitivity."

"His sensitivity manifested itself in many ways," wrote Steed. "First and foremost, though he eschewed regular hours and gainful employment for himself, he was always careful to see that his wife had a good job."

Another example he related was in reference to a bus picking him up at his home, for a trip to the state basketball tournament. As he boarded the bus, his wife said plaintively, "J.D., we don't have any stove wood cut." To which the Goat replied, in a tone so soft and suave that it could have been issued by Ronald Coleman, "Don't worry, honey, I ain't taking the axe."

CONTRARY TO WHAT most women maintain, men do often openly demonstrate their sensitivity and emotions. I recently heard an example that proves this:

"Why did you have to die, oh why did you have to die?" sobbed the gentleman as he hugged a tombstone in the cemetery.

"Your wife's grave?" asked a nearby lady sympathetically.

"No," he replied broken heartedly. "Her first husband's."

Lack of communication may be part of the problem. After living with the same woman for nigh on to 60 years, I find that interpreting what she means by a statement can change over the years. For example, "Light my fire" is not now a romantic invitation, but instead a request to light the gas logs in the fireplace by her chair.

It appears to me that too much sensitivity can be worse than too little. Too many folks nowadays become easily offended.

At a meeting in Atlanta, a lady from Tennessee boasted to me of how her husband never went to any meetings without asking her to go along. I didn't make any points with her when I replied, "He told me he'd rather take you with him, than have to kiss you goodbye."

MY FEELING IS THAT men in this country have let things get out of control. On a trip we took to Kenya a few years ago, I noted two native women busily building a hut in a rural area, while five men sat under a tree playing a game. In olden days, men there were hunters and warriors, while women stayed home and did all the work. Since hunting and fighting were no longer necessary, the men had decided that this division of responsibility was still a good idea.

And they call them primitive and less intelligent that we are!

However, I must admit that women are superior in some respects. For example, Fred Astaire received accolades for having been such a marvelous dancer. Yet his partner Ginger Rogers did the same steps, and did them on high heels and moving backwards.

And I also must admit that wives are often extremely helpful to their husbands. I recently heard a story about a wife who was perhaps too helpful:

"Have you ever been unfaithful to me?" asked her husband.

"Yes," she admitted, "but only for your benefit."

"How can your unfaithfulness be of benefit to me?"

"WELL, DO YOU REMEMBER when the bank was preparing to foreclose on our house mortgage? I slept with the bank president in order to get him not to do so. And do you remember when your boss was going to fire you, but then didn't? It's because I agreed to sleep with him also."

"In that case I can forgive you. Were there any other instances?"

"Well, yes," she replied. "Do you remember when you had your heart set on being elected president of your lodge, and you were 14 votes short?"

Jeepers! That Was Really a Hot 4th of July

July 2006

The lady discovered that it doesn't always pay to be nice by inviting friends to a wonderful Fourth of July picnic.

BEVERLY AND LEN WOODWARD sure can throw one heckuva Fourth of July party! Other Fourth of July hosts entertain their guests by exploding fireworks. The Woodwards instead exploded an entire automobile. To begin at the beginning.

"If you don't have any plans for the Fourth of July," Beverly phoned me the day before the Fourth, "would you like to join Vallie Orr, Betty Zane and Bill Morris, and Len and I for a picnic supper atop Simms Mountain, where we own some property?"

At the appointed time, we drove to the base of the mountain and parked the car. From there, the road to the top of the mountain was extremely steep, and could only generously be described as a road. Just a couple of ruts, with rocks and slick spots, and a bumpy ride. Len picked us up in his four-wheel-drive Jeep, since only four-wheelers could make it up the slope.

He had to make two trips to the top to accommodate all of us. Beverly and I were in the second group, along with chauffeur Len. About three-quarters of the way up, all of a sudden smoke came pouring out of the engine. We figured there was probably a leak in the radiator, and we decided we would wait until the engine cooled and then refill it with water to make the rest of the trip. In the meantime we got out and trudged the rest of the uphill way.

WE RELAXED IN THE SOLITUDE and serenity of a clearing in the forest, awaiting suppertime. Shortly thereafter, Len walked back down the hill to check on the car. On his return he told us, "I have some good news and bad news. The good news is that I have fire insurance on the Jeep." The bad news was, of course, that it was engulfed in flames.

"If we can just get down to the bottom of the hill," someone said after we commiserated with the Woodwards over the loss of the car, "at least we can get back to Rome in the car we left at the bottom."

"The problem with that," replied Beverly, "is that the keys for that car are in my purse, and my purse is in the burning Jeep." Along with Len's billfold.

Our other concern was that the blazing Jeep could start a forest fire since we have had such dry conditions. The Morris's had a cell phone, and they called 911 to notify the fire department. The 911 source that answered was in DeKalb County in Alabama. However, they obviously got the message to the fire department in Rome.

In the meantime, Len and Beverly rushed fixing a really great meal so that we could finish in time for a bunch of less-than-spring chickens to walk down the mountain before it got dark. Walking down such a steep slope wasn't exactly easy. But we managed to stumble, fumble, bumble, tumble, mumble and grumble (not to be confused with the law firm of the same name) our way down.

About half way, we ran into two Rome firemen on their way up to the burning Jeep with two fire extinguishers. I am certain that they now better appreciate riding to fires on a fire truck rather than toting 40-pound fire extinguishers up a mountain.

BY THEN THE FIRE had died down after completely obliterating the Jeep, and fortunately had not caught any of the nearby trees on fire. The fireman were great as they aided us with the rest of the descent to the bottom, where we arrived by dusk at the fire truck parked on the road with lights flashing, to the bewilderment of passing motorists.

They stayed with us until Jim and Missy Morris (Betty Zane and Bill's son and daughter-in-law) arrived in two cars to carry us back to civilization.

The moral of the story: It just doesn't pay to be a nice guy. The Woodwards went to a lot of work and trouble to entertain us and provide a great meal and relaxing atmosphere. And for their generosity, all they got was a burned-up car, plus a loss of all their credit cards, driver's licenses, etc. in the fire.

But they sure can provide an interesting party!

Only Sure Bet in Vegas Is Women Are 'Friendly'

September 2006

A country boy goes to Las Vegas. His adventures with the opposite sex while there.

ANGUS MCTAVISH PASSED AWAY. Since the newspaper charged by the word for obituary notices, his frugal widow instructed them to limit the notice to just three words, "Angus McTavish died."

"You're allowed six words for the minimum rate," the editor explained to her. "So you're entitled to three more words at no additional rate."

"Good," she replied. "Change it to read, 'Angus McTavish died. Oldsmobile for sale."

Like Mrs. McTavish, my bride is also of Scottish ancestry. However, over the years she has struggled valiantly to overcome the basic frugality of her ancestors; quite successfully I must sorrowfully add.

But in one respect her Scottish forefathers would be proud of her. She refuses to squander money on gambling.

If Georgia's schools were solely dependent on her purchase of lottery tickets, we'd soon be back to log cabin, dirt-floor schoolhouses.

Thus whenever I must attend a meeting in Las Vegas, she always elects to stay home. Besides, she knows she can trust me to behave. She knows I'm too decent, too honorable, and too old to get into trouble.

Anyway, this is a too-long preamble to explain why I was unaccompanied by spouse on two different trips to Las Vegas, and how this led to a couple of embarrassing experiences.

The first took place approximately 15 years ago on my first trip to Vegas. I was waiting in the lobby for a friend and his wife, who were taking me to dinner and a show.

I COULDN'T HELP but ogle, surreptitiously I thought, a good-looking female who was passing by. She caught me at it and immediately approached and started a conversation.

I may be a country boy, but it didn't take long for me to figure out it was her profession, rather than my good looks, that had instigated her advance.

(Like the story of the man who was greeted warmly by a buxom young lady in a restaurant. "She's just someone I know professionally," he stammered to his wife. "Whose profession?" asked his wife. "Yours or hers?"

A few minutes later my friends arrived. I was in a quandary. My dear old mother had done her best to teach me proper manners. However, she had never covered the subject of what is proper etiquette when you are talking to a prostitute and good friends approach.

I decided the only gentlemanly thing to do was to make introductions all around. Which I did. As we left, my friend whispered in my ear, "I don't believe it was necessary to introduce my wife to a prostitute."

This month I was again in Las Vegas for another meeting. On arrival at the airport I sat down next to a young lady in the baggage claim area as I waited for a friend to get his luggage.

"Hi. My name is Judy Lee. What's yours?" she asked.

ALL I COULD THINK OF was the immortal words of Yogi Berra when he said, "It's déjà vu all over again."

Thus I'm afraid I answered in a rather rude and unfriendly fashion, figuring I was again being solicited.

Fortunately I did not make some smart aleck remark like, "Your place or mine?" because I discovered after a few minutes' conversation that she was a very nice lady who was waiting there for her husband to pick up their luggage.

They had just arrived in Las Vegas to attend an auto-dealers convention. She had assumed I was part of their group, and was just being friendly.

Life was much simpler in the olden days when you didn't have to be suspicious of friendly strangers.

Nome, Hain't Fixin' to Start Talkin' Yankee

October 2006

When this Yankee moved South, he discovered that southern women talked funny.

"I'M REPAIRIN' TO GO to town," a native Georgian told his Yankee friend.

"You mean 'preparing,'" responded the Northener. "'Repairing' means 'to fix.'"

"That's what I said. I'm fixin' to go to town."

I must confess that many years ago, I would have been just as confused as the Yankee in this old joke. Born and raised in northern Illinois, I was also a Yankee before having the good fortune to move to Rome.

Spending a good bit of time in the South Pacific during World War II showed me that it isn't absolutely necessary to freeze one's rear end during the winter months. Hence the wise decision to move south after completing my schooling.

Although I have come to thoroughly enjoy the colorful, melodic and friendly Southern accent and idiom, in addition to 'fixin' there were many other terms that were perplexing to my bride at first.

Summers—"I know that boy is around here summers."

Tarred—"Ah'm too tarred to go out tonight."

War—"Be careful. Don't get stuck on that barb war."

Tar arn—"You can't change a flat tar without a tar arn."

Toreckly—"You go ahead. I'll be along toreckly."

Bidness—"It's none of your business."

Ratcheer—"I left my car keys ratcheer, and now they're gone."

Airs—"That shortstop done made two airs already."

Idinit—"Mighty hot today, idinit?""HOW DO YOU get to Chattanooga?" asked the lost tourist trying to get directions from an elderly gentleman rocking on his front porch.

"Wal, mostly my son-in-law carries me," the old man replied. This use of the word "carry" to indicate driving someone somewhere, rather than physically carrying him, was also at first difficult to understand.

Different words being unintentionally pronounced the same also threw me for awhile. On a "Candid Camera" show I saw, the announcer asked a gentleman from South Carolina, "How do you pronounce the word 'f-a-r'?"

"Fahr," he replied.

"How do you pronounce the word 'f-i-r-e'?" he then asked.

"Fahr," was again the response.

"Then those two words are pronounced just the same?" asked the announcer.

"No, no!" he responded fervently. "'F-a-r' is pronounced 'fahr' and 'f-i-r-e' is pronounced 'fahr'!"

Or the story of the two Yankee women driving south who stopped to get gas atop a mountain in Tennessee on a clear, crisp day. "Just smell that air," one of them said as she took a deep breath.

"That 'ere what?" asked the elderly gas station

attendant.

Another advantage of "talkin' Southern" is how it doesn't take nearly as much effort because it often reduces the number of syllables in a word.

Cain't—cannot

Jev-ver—did you ev-er

Cocola—co-ca co-la

Nome—No ma'am

Zackly—ex-act-ly

Cyst—as-sist

Prolly—pro-ba-bly

The two prize winners are one syllable words that replace four syllables:

Spear—su-per-i-or

Nairn—nar-y a oneHOWEVER, I MUST ADMIT after all these, one thing still baffles me. When so many Southern words efficiently reduce the number of syllables, why do a few instead add syllables?

Day-um—"Frankly my dear, I don't give a day-um."

Fay-an—"It was so hot I had to turn on the electric fay-un."

Gri-yuts—"I have gri-yuts for breakfast every morning."

Pay-an—"I'll sign it if you hand me that pay-un."

Shay-um—It's a shay-um that with the numbers of Yankees who, like me, have wised up and moved south, this Southern accent is becoming less prevalent.

I've "axed" why from a "right smart" of folks, but "nairn" seemed to be able to "hep" or "cyst" me.

Making Decisions Sure Easier with a Wife

November 2006

This was written during the couple of years I was a widower, and discovered how difficult it is to have to make my own decisions.

IT SEEMS KIND of strange that my life has become so much more complicated as a result of becoming a widower. With the demise of wife Mary one year ago, I now for the first time in my life have to make my own decisions—such as where to go, what to wear, how to act, and even what I like and what I think!

I just don't have the experiential background to handle the pressure of making such decisions.

During my childhood and teen years, I was subject to parental authority. The next few years I was under the domination of the U.S. Navy, an organization not particularly noted for giving its members freedom of thought and action.

Then, at war's end, I got married. Husband's having "decision making authority" during marriage is pretty well described by an old country song. I don't remember the exact words, but its message was a husband's lament that went something like this:

"When we got married, the preacher asked her, 'Do you take this man as your lawful wedded husband?'

She said, 'I do.'

"Then he asked me, 'Do you take this woman as your lawful wedded wife?' and she said, 'He do.' I figured right about then that I wasn't going to have a lot of control over my life."

"WHAT KIND OF GRITS do you want me to buy for you?" my aforementioned bride once asked me.

"Just plain grits," I replied.

"Are you sure? I figured you'd rather have flavored grits."

"No, just plain grits."

"If I could eat grits, I'd rather have the flavored kind. Are you sure you wouldn't rather have them?"

By that time I figured it would be easier just to eat flavored grits.

Bill Cosby gives another example of this lack of husbandly authority:

"We were out to dinner one night. The hostess passed the dish of potatoes for those who wanted a second helping. My wife said, "Bill doesn't want any more potatoes."

After these many years of depending on my bride's admittedly superior fashion sense, another decision I must now make is, "Which tie goes with this suit?" I am happy to report that I am handling this quite admirably. According to daughters and granddaughters, I am batting almost .500 in this department.

I also no longer have someone to point out my inadequacies and wrongdoings in order to enhance my chances for self-improvement.

I HAVE ALWAYS had an unfortunate propensity for gravitationally depositing food stuffs on my wearing apparel when I'm dining out. Invariably this was pointed out to me by my bride in an attempt to make me more cautious in the future.

However, I have not seemed to improve in this regard over the years, and probably easily qualify for membership in the Slim Likelihood Of Betterment Society (SLOBS for short.)

Despite no longer receiving such self-improvement and decision-making advice, I do find that in some ways life has become easier. For the first time in my life I have control of the thermostat and TV volume settings. And I have advanced from owning approximately 16.3 percent of available closet space, to now having 100 percent.

Also, no longer do I have to be concerned as to whether I leave the toilet seat up or not. I believe it was Rodney Dangerfield who said, "There's no satisfying my wife. First she complained because I left the toilet seat up. So I put it down. Now she complains about having to sit on a wet toilet seat."

I DON'T BELIEVE I'd have had the guts to say that. Although I did survive one similar slip up a few years back. My helpmate walked across the room carrying a broom. Without stopping to consider the possible repercussions, I asked her, "Going for a ride?"

Do you know what's really strange? How such matrimonial memories can be happy and sad at the same time.

An Education about Female Peculiarities

January 2007

In which I give the benefit of my wisdom about women, acquired over MANY years, to my new grandson-in-law. Only to discover I really hadn't acquired any wisdom on the subject!

MY GRANDDAUGHTER JENNIFER was married recently. He's a good guy, definitely a "keeper." I hope they have a long and happy marriage. In order for that to come about, her new husband must learn, and adapt to, the idiosyncrasies of womankind.

Thus I shall herewith give him the benefit of my wisdom on the subject, based on personal experience with one wife, three daughters, and four granddaughters.

My greatest regret is that Jennifer's grandmother, who doubled as my wife, passed away before having the opportunity to witness the wedding. However, her demise does allow me greater freedom to give a more frank and complete appraisal of the peculiarities of womanly behavior without fear of matrimonial doghouse repercussions. Such peculiarities include:

Females have amazing, but selective memories.

Looking into the future, let's assume you have now been married for 25 years. This means you have had 25 anniversaries and 25 birthdays to remember in some way. Let us further assume that you "done good" and remembered 49. Which do you think she is going to remember, the 49 successes or one miss?

This memory trait has been noted by many men much wiser than I.

"My wife is afflicted with total recall," was S. J. Perelman's observation.

"Even more important than remembering birthdays and anniversaries, is remembering what happened the time you were supposed to remember a day and failed to do so," said George Burns.

I think husbands should be forgiven for forgetting their mistakes. After all, there is no sense in two people remembering the same thing.

You can't win.

No matter what action you take, you'll find that it's probably the wrong one. Even when you really are trying to be nice.

I was recently able to establish contact, via the internet, with a shipmate from World War II. He had retained, and sent me a copy of our ship's newsletter from April 16, 1945. In it appeared the following item:

"Mrs. Ester G. McKane is not too happy about the Nazi flag her husband sent her from Germany. The swastika-decorated emblem smelled of disinfectant, so she hung it on the backyard clothesline. Complaints started coming in on the telephone. Passerby threatened to tear it down. 'We are airing it, not flying it,' she answered the complaints. 'I wish the stupid thing was back in Germany!'"

So much for the poor guy who thought he was being thoughtful in sending her a valuable souvenir.

Female logic is not only difficult to understand, but

even more difficult to refute.

This trait is either inborn or learned at an early age.

"Eat your squash or you can't have any dessert!" I thundered at daughter Janet as she toyed with her food when she was about four years old.

"I don't like squash," she pouted.

"Why don't you like it?"

"Because I have never tried it before."

Just how are you going to argue with female logic like that?

Another example:

"The car won't start," a lady phoned her husband. "It has water in the carburetor."

"Where is the car?" her mate inquired.

"In the lake."

It is not only just recently that the conflicting views of women and men have been noted. The 16th century French philosopher Montaigne once said, "A good marriage would join a blind wife and a deaf husband."

Space does not permit me to further explore the subject at this time. Thus Brandon (the grandson-in-law) shall have to wait for the next installment for further advice. Unless I am rubbed out by the WSPFW (Women's Society for Preservation of Feminine Wiles) which is dedicated to the goal of keeping males confused.

Idiosyncrasies of Female Mind

February 2007

"Why do you treat me like this after I gave you the best years of my life?" sobbed the wife.

"If those were the best ones, I sure as hell am glad I didn't have to spend the rest of them with you!"

Hopefully my advice can prevent this from happening.

YOU MAY RECALL, if you were paying attention, that my previous literary effort concerned giving advice to my new grandson-in-law (Brandon) on how to adapt to the idiosyncrasies of females. Following is further knowledge and advice he may find helpful.

Turnabout is not fair play.

I have never been able to figure out why it's OK for a wife to tell her husband he's getting fat, but he's in a whole heap of trouble if he tells her the same thing! Even retroactively.

A couple of years ago, a granddaughter lost a few pounds and looked great. So I thought I would please her by telling her so. "You look great since you lost a few pounds!" I told her. "You were getting just a little chunky before."

Far from being complimented, she answered, "You should never tell a female she used to be a little chunky."

Hair is another illustration of how honesty is not always the best policy in dealing with females. Women seem to have a pathological preoccupation with their hair, a preoccupation not shared with the same unwholesome fervor by males. Therefore it is unwise to give a straight answer when asked by your wife, "How do you like my hair?"

It may take awhile but they'll get even for your transgressions.

Witness the case of the gentleman who was brought to trial before the honorable Judge Walter Matthews charged with stealing a can of peaches.

"How many peaches were in the can?" the judge asked.

"Four," he replied.

"Ok, one day in jail for each peach you stole."

"Your Honor," interjected the man's wife, still smoldering from her husband having again forgotten her birthday and anniversary. "He also stole a can of peas."

Don't be too handy around the house.

If you screw up enough household projects, you'll soon find that you will no longer be requested to do them. Thus you'll find yourself out playing golf or tennis, while your "smarter" friends are at home doing household tasks.

Always complain bitterly.

Even about chores you don't really mind doing. This helps establish more "points" than if you did them willingly. Such as yard work. I do hope my late bride never discovers that I find I really enjoy the yard work about which I so bitterly complained.

There is another advantage to this making a fool of yourself griping about certain activities. For example I hate shopping. During the first years of our marriage, I became so insufferable whenever embarked on a shopping trip, that I was soon no longer asked to go with her.

If you're not careful you'll find women will take charge.

This is another trait that is learned early on. Gwen Sirmans tells of her three-year-old son Knox announcing, "I'm going to marry Cappie."

"How do you know?" she asked.

"Because Cappie told me so."

"I'm hot," Jeff Foxworthy reports his wife told him in the middle of the night during their second year of marriage. "So I got up to turn on the ceiling fan. On the way back to bed, it dawned on me, 'Whoa. Why am I doing this? I'm not hot!'"

You must be careful what you say.

One couple reportedly decided they must both forego all luxuries in order to overcome their financial difficulties.

"I can't believe you bought a case of beer when we agreed to cut out all frills," said the wife.

"Well, I'm not the only one. This bill says you bought $80 worth of cosmetics."

"That's different. I bought them so I can look beautiful for you."

"Well, that's what the beer was for, too," he unwisely responded.

DESPITE ALL THESE PROBLEMS I think you'll thoroughly enjoy being married. Like the guy who said, "I love being married. I was single a long time, and at social affairs I got really tired of having to finish my own sentences, and count my own drinks."

Speaking French All Greek to Him

May 2007

In which I discover that trying to communicate in France, based on having one year of high school French, can get you in trouble with a wife.

MANY YEARS AGO an Italian boxer named Primo Carnera came to this country in order to train for a boxing match for the world championship. "I can't tell him nothin' straight," complained the Brooklyn trainer assigned to him. "All he can speak is Eye-talion, French, and Spanish. It's a shame he ain't smart enough to speak English!"

When I read about this recently, it reminded me of the troubles I've also had in the past communicating with "furriners."

The first column I ever wrote for the *Rome News-Tribune* some 25 years ago gave a couple of examples of such difficulties. In it I told of a trip to Paris where I quickly discovered that having had two years of high school French does not exactly make one proficient in the language. Sentences I had learned, such as, "La crayon est sur la table" (the pencil is on the table) I found to be rather difficult to work into any conversation. And if I showed off my knowledge of French by saying "Comment allez vous?" (how are you?), the person I was addressing would assume I spoke French, and would let loose a torrent of unintelligible (to me) verbiage in response.

WIFE MARY AND I on the first day went to a small café for lunch. Since she had not had the benefit of high school French, I told her she could relax and let me take care of the ordering. The problem was that the only thing I could interpret on the menu was "Hamburger du Cheval." "Hamburger" was rather easy to translate, and I recalled that "cheval" was the French word for "cheese." So I told her that's what she needed to order if she'd like a cheeseburger.

When the order came, there was a fried egg atop the burger rather than cheese, but she decided to eat it anyway. About the time she finished the last bite, I suddenly remembered that actually the French word for cheese is "fromage", and that "cheval" was unfortunately the word for horse. I finally summoned the courage to casually mention this to her, hoping that she would find it mildly amusing. She didn't!!!

French friends later told us that "hamburger du cheval" is a beef hamburger, with an egg riding on top like a jockey. However, I think she still was convinced that I had caused her to consume a horseburger.

THAT EVENING WE WENT TO a restaurant. My fluency recognized the word "vin" on the menu as being the word for "wine." So I ordered a glass. Except somehow what I got was large pitcher of vin. This presented a few problems. First, it was very good. Secondly, I was raised during the depression with the constant admonition from my mother, "Finish your meal! The poor starving children in India would love to have what you have left on your plate and in your glass." Although to be perfectly honest, my teetotaling mother undoubtedly had milk, rather than wine, in mind.

The third problem is best illustrated by the story of the drunk who was hailed before the judge who asked him, "How did you get in this deplorable condition?"

"It was bad company I was in that caused it, Judge. There were four of us with a quart of whiskey, and the other three don't drink." I had the same problem because my wife didn't drink. Even so, somehow the entire content of the pitcher had disappeared by the completion of the meal. I vaguely recall floating happily back to the hotel

BUT EVEN WHEN A PERSON speaks another language fluently, there can still be problems in meaning, due to their not understanding the common usage and idioms of the other language. I am on the Comite Scientifique de Lecture for a French optical journal, Points de Vue, which is published in four languages. Much as I hate to admit it, the position is not nearly as prestigious as it sounds. All I've ever had to do is to check the English translations to make certain of proper word usage.

One such article recently referred to "Primitive" Health Care. Which immediately gave me visions of a witch doctor's dance and incantations. Then it dawned on me what the author was describing instead was "Primary" Health Care. The translator had used the definition of "primitive" in the dictionary which read "primary, or basic, or initial."

Another time I received an email from a French lady thanking me for my precious help. Now I've been called a lot of things during my life, but never before had I been labeled as "precious." I finally figured she meant "valuable", which is one of the definitions of "precious."

"I DON'T KNOW WHY you have so much trouble communicating with the French," a friend told me. "It's obviously an easy language to learn. It's so simple that when I when I was in France, I noticed that even two year old kids could speak it."

A Nomenclature for Laughter

August 2007

"I think I'm gonna divorce my wife. She ain't spoke to me in over two months," said Bubba to Earl as they sat in their boat fishing.

"Better think it over. Women like that are hard to find."

But if they ARE talking, best you listen carefully to what they're saying.

AUTHOR WILL STANTON tells of meeting at a party a British lady who had purchased a neighboring farm with a very old home on it.

"Are you enjoying your new home?" he asked.

"Very much," said the lady. "We have ghosts, you know."

"No," he replied, "I didn't. It's funny I've never heard about them before."

"Well, they weren't there before. We brought them with us."

"We had one in the house when I was a boy," responded Stanton in an attempt to humor the lady's obvious belief in ghosts. "I could hear it in the attic. Sometimes it would even come in my room."

"And it didn't bother you?"

"Oh, no," said Stanton. "I've always been quite fond of them."

Just then the lady's husband came up. After introducing him, she said to her husband, "Mr. Stanton and I have been having the most extraordinary conversation about goats!"

A MISUNDERSTANDING of the names of persons or things can often cause a whole heap of trouble.

Another illustration is the Wgasa Monorail at the San Diego Wild Animal Park. When the monorail was first built, authorities decided they wanted a jazzy African sounding name for it, so they emailed all their employees asking for suggestions.

One of the replies was just one word, "WGASA". The authorities loved its African sound, so adopted it as the monorail's name. It was much later they discovered that what the employee meant with his reply was not a suggested name, but instead a crude acronym for, "Who gives a s___ anyway." (This has been verified as a true story. Not to imply that other things I impart to you are not necessarily true.)

WHEN THE LATE BILLY MCWILLIAMS and I and our wives accompanied the Shorter College Chorale on their tour of Spain and France a few years ago, I heard that as he and Maggie entered a French restaurant, the head waiter greeted them, "Bon appetit."

"McWilliams," replied Billy.

"You idiot," said his wife Maggie. "He wasn't giving you his name. 'Bon appetit' means 'I hope you enjoy your meal.'"

After dinner as they left, Billy said to the waiter, "Bon appetit."

"McWilliams," replied the waiter.

ANOTHER NAME PROBLEM COMES about when inappropriate names are joined together in marriage. One example I read about—When a guy named Joe Hardy married Shelley Harr, the headline above the story of the wedding in their newspaper read, "Hardy-Harr."

Even worse was when Peter Best married Judy Lay. The headline appearing just above the photo of the sweet and lovely bride read, "Best-Lay."

ONE NAME THAT I do not at the moment view with hearty approval after what he did to me, is my good friend, Dave McCorkle, or rather my "former friend" Dave McCorkle. When I shamelessly boasted to him about having read in the *Rome News-Tribune* that my column had received a third place award in the National Newspaper Association Better Newspaper Contest, he replied:

"It's probably like the story I recently read, about the lady who was a lousy cook, but nonetheless baked a cake and entered it at the County Fair. She was delighted when she was informed that she had been awarded the ribbon for third place. Until she discovered that hers was the only entry in the contest."

Billy Jo, aka Jack, Is a Man on the Move

October, 2007

For a brief period following my first wife's demise, and before I married WHN, I was for the first time in my life King of the Castle.

I NEED TO SQUELCH a scurrilous rumor. Everyone assumes that when "AKA" is used in conjunction with someone's name, it indicates that the person is a hardened criminal who uses an alias. Such as "George Jones, AKA 'Bugsy' Jones," or "Jack Martin, AKA 'Jack The Ripper.'"

Thus it was rather disconcerting a few weeks ago to read in the *Rome News-Tribune* Roman Record of a transaction which stated that, "William John Runninger, AKA Jack Runninger" had purchased a new home. This, in addition to my new home being in the vicinity of the jail, has caused some wiseass friends to circulate the rumor that I have moved INTO the jail, rather than its neighborhood.

The real reason I moved near the jail is that I figured I'd have a better class of neighbors there, than those I had at my previous dwelling, such reprobates as McDougald, Wilcox, Fambro, Kelley, Yancey, Ward, Doss, Gray, Nordeman, Matthews, Betz, Edwards, Green, Reynolds, Wilkins, Williams, Youmans, Griffin,

Kiefer, Bennett, et al.

MY NEW HOME IS the very first I've ever inhabited where I am King of the Castle. The fact that I am its only occupant perhaps has something to do with this.

"I've had bad luck with both my wives," a man told me. "The first one left me, and the second one didn't."

In contrast I had only one marriage which lasted for 60 years prior to my wife's demise. 48 of those 60 years were spent in the residence I've just abdicated. It will come as no surprise to other husbands that I somehow never there felt I had control of that household.

"AFTER I GOT MARRIED, I learned that I needed a lot of things I never knew I needed," wrote the late columnist, Lewis Grizzard. "Ten zillion houseplants, for instance. *Plants?* In the hallways, my wife has planted a couple of *trees*. The kids want me to build them a tree house in one of them." I found the same problem at my house.

It appears to me that if the Lord wanted plant life to reside indoors, he would have planted it there rather than outdoors. But I found over the years that I felt I was gradually being squeezed out as more and more jungle took over my indoor territory.

Being a female, I find that daughter Star, who is now my household manager, is also obsessed with inundating me with plant life that takes up space that I wish to personally occupy. However this is no longer a problem since as soon as she leaves I can move the foliage out of the way. (Incidentally, moving to a new residence would have been even more traumatic if it had not been for her and daughter Nancy's help!

NOW THAT I AM master of my domain, I have chosen

as my decor motif for my new abode the Early Lower Slobbovian Period, in which beauty and neatness are secondary to comfort and convenience.

Thus for the very first time, my exercise bicycle sits smack in the middle of the living room so that I can watch TV while using it. And the cereal boxes stay on the kitchen table full time, since putting them up in a cabinet after breakfast only necessitates hauling them out again the following morning.

"What did you do before you got married?" I once asked an acquaintance.

"Anything I wanted to!" he replied.

Self-Professed Wallflower Protests Too Much?

November 2007

The lad was having trouble finding a wife. Every time he brought a prospective bride home, his momma didn't like her. Finally he found a girl friend exactly like his mother. His father didn't like that one.

My mother didn't have that problem. During courtship of girls during my early years, Don Juan I was not.

IN GOING THROUGH an accumulation of photos, clippings, etc. in the process of moving, I came across a newspaper photograph. It appeared in the Indianapolis Star newspaper in 1943.

"The popular man surrounded by ten DePauw beauties," read the caption under the photo, "is Jack Runninger, president of Kappa Tau Kappa which this Saturday will choose a queen to reign over its' interfraternity ball."

This description of me being popular with the fairer sex was a big fat lie!

Instead of the photo triggering a pleasant memory, all it did was painfully remind me of what a klutz I was in courting the fairer sex during my college years.

DePauw University was noted as a school of poor boys (including me) and rich girls. The tuition was expensive, but half of us males were there on a full ride Rector Scholarship, while no scholarships were offered to females. (Expensive back then meant that the tuition at DPU cost the grand sum of $250 per year! In comparison, the U. of Illinois tuition was $60 per year.)

So here was a ready opportunity for me to marry into a rich family, and spend the balance of my life in the lap of luxury. But unfortunately these sophisticated young ladies scared hell out of me. So I spent the Saturday night dating nights shooting baskets at the gym with friends.

UPPERCLASSMEN IN MY FRATERNITY decided this did not reflect well on the fraternity's social image, so they arranged for me a date with a very pretty fellow freshman named Sue Pulliam. The date was not a great success. She obviously was not smitten by my charm or good looks, or lack thereof, and it was clear that she was not interested in pursuing any future relationship. If only I had been more dashing and suave, I could have had it made:

Her father was the wealthy owner of the *Indianapolis Star* newspaper. She had an older sister who was also attending DPU, named Corrinne Pulliam. Corrinne was dating another student named James Quayle, whom she later married after graduation. They sired a son by the name of Dan Quayle, who as you recall became Vice President of the United States. If I had only been more lovable, I might have ended up married to his aunt and, as his "uncle in law," hobnobbed with the rich and famous in Washington.

But instead—back to the gym on Saturday nights.

BY MY SOPHOMORE YEAR I had gained slightly more sophistication and was perhaps a little more "couth." I imagined myself as older and more worldly than the incoming freshman girls, so was not quite as intimidated. In fact, I became somewhat smitten with one of them, and was able to garner a few dates with her.

Then came the night of my fraternity dance. Via nefarious schemes, I was able to get her alone later in the evening to attempt a little "necking" as it was called in those days. Come to think of it, I believe "necking" probably got its' name from the fact that it involved serious bodily contact only from the neck up.

Going to all the trouble of arranging the "aloneness" was a complete waste of time. I could have received a warmer response to my advances from an Eskimo's icebox, and that was the end of that relationship. So again I took my bruised ego back to the gym on Saturday nights.

FORTUNATELY BEFORE I COULD bruise it further, the US Navy decided that, rather than my remaining in college, they were in desperate need of my assistance in fighting the Japanese. I doubt there were many tears shed by the female students at my departure.

Wives Are the Better Half for Punch Lines

December, 2007

From Boogar Hollow, there's also the one about ole Doc Adams examining Mrs. Bodiah. Worried about her being so sick, he sez, "I don't like yo' wife's look, Mr. Bodiah."

"Well Doc," sez ole man Bodiah, "I ain't too crazy about her looks neither, but she is right good to me 'n the kids."

"WHY DO YOU GIVE women in general, and your wife in particular, such a hard time?" a lady asked me after a recent column.

It does seem sort of strange, but I find I enjoy kidding my wife even after she's passed away. Possibly because it makes it seem a little more like she's still here.

But it seems hardly fair that someone as attractive and irresistible as I, should receive such admonishment, while other males get away with statements more disrespectful of womankind.

RODNEY DANGERFIELD GETS paid for insulting women. A couple of his quips:

"I haven't spoken to my wife for 20 months. I don't like to interrupt her."

"In the beginning, God created earth and rested. Then God created man and rested. Then God created woman. Since then, neither God nor man has rested."

Even the "loser," Leroy, in the "Born Loser" comic strip, gets away with insults better than do I. A couple of his zingers:

"Your dress fits you like a glove," says Leroy to wife Loretta. "It sticks out in five places."

"Sure, we don't spend much time together," again to wife Loretta. "Why mess up something that works?"

THE GENTLE RED SKELTON even once gave tips for a happy marriage, which included:

"Twice a week, we go to a nice restaurant, have a little beverage, then comes good food and companionship. She goes on Tuesdays, I go on Fridays."

"We also sleep in separate beds. Hers is in Ontario and mine is in Tucson."

"I asked my wife where she wanted to go for our anniversary. 'Somewhere I haven't been in a long time.' she said. So I suggested the kitchen."

LONG-TIME ROMANS may remember in 1968 when Cedartown professional golfer, Doug Sanders, brought a number of Hollywood luminaries to Rome for a golf exhibition and to give a show at the city auditorium that night. The group included Andy Williams, Dean Martin, and Phil Harris.

As I followed Martin and Harris on the golf course, I noted the frequency with which they were taking nips from airline miniature bourbon bottles. By the time of the evening show, they were both pretty well snockered. Thus Martin's entire contribution to the show was to recite a poem, after which he tottered off the stage:

I have a new girl friend,
I could not love her more.

She's deaf and dumb and oversexed,
And owns a liquor store.

MY PERSONAL FAVORITE is author and attorney Robert Steed, who once wrote on his 25th wedding anniversary:

"It is difficult, painful, and almost impossible to believe that 25 years ago my apprehensive parents gave my hand in matrimony to the swarthy, suspect, and sexually precocious Linda Ruth McElroy in a simple but tasteful double ring ceremony. Polite society in west Georgia was, in a word, aghast. Not since Edward VIII renounced the throne to marry the American commoner, Wallis Simpson, had there been such an egregious mismatch across social and class boundaries.

"In the traditional engagement story reported dutifully by the society editor of the *Bowdon Bulletin,* the anxious mother of the bride-to-be, obviously grateful at the prospect that the fortuitous match might spare her dark and enigmatic daughter from an otherwise certain life of selling scuppernongs from the back of a pickup truck or reading palms in a dingy trailer, replied to a reporter's question as to when the nuptials would take place by blurting, 'There'll be no nuptials until after the wedding!'

"Through the intervening years the social, class, and intellectual differences have grown more, rather than less, acute and recurring questions repeated by one and all are, 'What does he see in her? Why are they together?' Certainly elements of habit, inertia, lust, nostalgia, a long-standing dread of alimony, and the stark possibility of being awarded custody of the children all play a part in this inexplicable but remarkably durable union."

I rest my case.

On a Mission to Expose Male Chauvinists

January 2008

A husband and wife were Christmas shopping, when all of a sudden she noticed that he had disappeared. She called him on his cell phone and angrily demanded, "Where have you gone?"

"Do you remember that jewelry store we were in a couple of hours ago, that had the diamond earrings you loved so much?"

"Oh yes!" she replied contritely.

"Well, I'm in the bar next door to it."

I would never do anything like this, yet I never seem to receive credit for my battles against chauvinism.

ONCE AGAIN I HAVE BEEN harshly judged. All because of a misunderstanding of my last column which described some of the foibles of females.

Ladies who have criticized me for it failed to note that none of the views about females in that column originated with me. I would personally not stoop so low to make such disparaging remarks about women. All of the quotes were from other men, not me. I delineated them only to expose these chauvinists. I agree that their comments were reprehensible and uncalled for. As a further service to my female friends, I shall hereby expose a few more deplorable comments from males who are not nearly as enlightened on the subject of women's rights as am I.

THIS VILIFYING OF WOMANKIND has been going on far too long! Even highly admired male figures are at times remiss in their comments about women. For example, Mark Twain once described his mother as a kindly and compassionate soul, who always warmed the water before drowning the kittens.

"Oh, Bill won't have any more," Bill Cosby's wife told the hostess at a dinner party when he was asked if he'd like a second helping of mashed potatoes. "Does she presume that I haven't mastered the art of thinking for myself?" remonstrated Cosby, demonstrating a distressing lack of appreciation for her gracious help in running his life.

"IT IS SAD TO REALIZE," said author Robert Steed in besmirching his wife, "that except for a teenage olfactory disorder that caused me to confuse the aroma of her lavishly applied Evening In Paris, with pure passion, I could have avoided being trapped in this bleak and interminable union."

"Women seem to have a pathological preoccupation with their hair, not shared with the same unwholesome fervor by males," was another despicable comment from Steed.

Henny Youngman should be horsewhipped for his uncalled for remarks about his wife's cooking:

"My wife dresses to kill. She cooks the same way."

And:

"My wife's cooking is so bad, the flies got together to raise enough money to patch the holes in the screen door."

"You don't want to get married because you're our only daughter?" comedian Sam Levenson quotes his father as saying to his daughter. "And you don't want to leave Mama behind to take care of such a large family by herself? Who are we to stand in the way of your happiness? You can take Mama with you."

AGAIN MY PURPOSE in quoting these males is not because I agree with them! Au contraire, my purpose is only to expose and criticize such chauvinism.

But, Ladies, you could be a big help in my campaign to stamp out male chauvinism. All you have to do is to revert to the rules of etiquette for women from the 19th century. Paying attention to manuals of advice from that era, and putting into practice what they say, will go a long way towards getting rid of male mudslinging. Such rules as:

HOW TO BE A BETTER WIFE (1897)

1. Start each day with a cheerful countenance and pleasant conversation.
2. Turn the harsh utterances of a scolding tongue into kind and gentle words.
3. Learn to bake juicy fruit pies and do so frequently.
4. Smooth out the wrinkles in your brow by thinking serene thoughts.
5. Do not interrupt your husband when he is speaking, thinking, or reading.

Also advised were the following traits:

- » Steadfastness in the face of hard work.
- » Obedience.
- » Pleasantness at mealtimes.
- » Lilting laughter.
- » Strength of character, arms, legs, back.

Together we can win this war against male chauvinism if you'll but adhere to these principles.

Weddings Are Fragile as Glass

May 2008

Getting hitched wasn't easy. Maybe the cab driver was right?

RECENTLY IN THESE PAGES, my friend Sam Garner wrote of the difficulties encountered in getting married while serving in the Navy during World War II. I wish to hereby second the motion.

Back in July of 1945, after having participated in the invasions of Iwo Jima and Okinawa, my ship was sent back to the United States for repairs, in preparation for the scheduled fall invasion of Japan. Since we would be in the Richmond shipyards (in San Francisco Bay) for almost two weeks, fiancée Mary Gibson and I decided this would be a good opportunity to tie the knot.

Thus she and future mother-in-law arrived in San Francisco by train the day after our ship arrived, and registered at a hotel there, some 20 to 30 miles from the shipyards. Although I had to stand shipboard watch the first six days, I was scheduled to have the following six days on leave, so that we could get hitched and go on a brief honeymoon.

WHEN THE FIRST DAY of my six day leave arrived, I was to pick her and future mother-in-law up at their hotel, then proceed by cab to the little chapel at which she had made wedding arrangements. After the wedding, Momma-in-law would go to the train station to return home, and we would go to the fancy Mark Hopkins Hotel, arranged for us by the USO for the one night. Then for a four day honeymoon at nearby romantic Mud Lake.

Sounds simple enough. But to get to their hotel, I had to first take a cab from the shipyards to Richmond, to catch the interurban train to San Francisco. When I reached for my billfold to pay the cab driver, I discovered I had left it on the ship. So—cab back to the ship, get billfold, return to train stop, and board the next train. As the train pulled away, I glanced out the window. Just in time to get a horrifying view of the suitcase I had inadvertently left sitting by the tracks. So—off at the first station, return train to original site, get suitcase, and reboard the next train.

FINALLY I ARRIVED at the hotel, and picked up future bride and mother-in-law. Plus a #$%@?& glass serving plate. A college friend of hers had presented it to her as a wedding present the previous day. The sucker was heavy, and was more than 24" in diameter, and thus would not fit in a suitcase. Which necessitated me carrying it everywhere we went. My big mistake was in not dropping and breaking it right then.

With all this, I was almost beginning to agree with our cab driver, who on the way to the chapel kept telling me I was making a big mistake. "I've had bad luck with three wives," he told us. "The first two left me, and the the third one won't."

The following day, my bride, I, and the #$%@?& glass

plate in my lap, proceeded by bus to the aforementioned honeymoon site, Mud Lake. Unfortunately, the site's name was pretty much descriptive of its beauty.

THERE ANOTHER PROBLEM arose. I was at the macho period of my life, and was innocent, and stupid, enough to envision a "Me Tarzan, you Jane" male dominant relationship in our marriage. However this 5' 2'', 100 pounder evidently didn't understand this, and continually beat the stew out of me playing ping pong, thereby destroying my macho image.

Although I doubt our wedding had much to do with it, the atomic bomb was dropped on Hiroshima during our honeymoon, and a few days later the war ended. Unfortunately by then my ship and I were headed back to the South Pacific, although fortunately just for occupation purposes rather than invasion. I finally returned to San Francisco in November, and my bride and I headed by train to Great Lakes Naval station in Illinois (with the #$%@$/ plate again perched in my lap).

By then, the #$%@? plate had spent a whole lot more time in my lap, than had my bride.

Even When Employees Are Nice, Don't Think Shopping Fun

June 2008

One would think that this episode during my courtship of the lady, would have warned me that life was going to be complicated if I married this lady. However love conquers all.

I WOULD SUGGEST THAT if you ever get an invitation to go shopping with a lady by the name of Helen Cobb, that you run, not walk, for the nearest exit. The lady is a jinx.

I base this warning on a recent shopping excursion I made with her: What happened was, I had resigned my membership in Sam's Club, and discovered I needed some items I had been purchasing there.

"SINCE YOU HAVE A Sam's card," I phoned the aforementioned Mrs. Cobb, "how about letting me go with you next time you go to Sam's?" Incidentally, I rediscovered during this conversation the distressing attribute of ALL females to place the blame for anything that goes wrong, on the nearest male present.

In the middle of our conversation, the phone went dead. When I called her back, fellow males will not be surprised that her first words were not "What happened?" but instead, "What did you do?"

Anyway she agreed to my accompanying her, and we arrived at the counter with our respective (or as Dizzy Dean used to say, "respectable") purchases. She planned to pay for her share with a check, and I was paying for mine with cash. The first problem arose. She had inadvertently brought the Sam's card for Network Day Service Center, of which she is the director, rather than her personal card.

"Charges on this card are automatically billed to the Center, so you cannot pay for them with cash or check," the clerk informed her. Somehow I didn't think that Network would be too enthralled to discover that they had purchased vitamins, grapefruit and strawberries for me. The clerk called in a couple of other employees to have a conference on what to do.

YOU KNOW HOW IT IS at the grocery store, for example. You have completed your shopping and are trying to decide which of the three open checkout lines you should select. You realize it really doesn't matter which one you choose, because it will turn out to be the wrong one anyway. Sure enough, the person in front of you in the line you pick has some sort of problem. This requires the tracking down of two assistant managers, and finally the manager to come to the counter to sort out the matter. All of which seemingly takes no longer than 30 minutes.

During this time, you watch other shoppers breeze quickly through the lines you did not choose. Some of these shoppers had not even entered the store to begin shopping while you were already standing in the molasses line. Some probably hadn't even yet left home. But finally the matter is solved, and the lady is told her correct charge. Only then does she begin to look in the convoluted snarl of multitudinous items in a purse as large as a suitcase, for her checkbook. After a ten minute search she finally finds it, and then laboriously begins to fill out all the items on the check, most of which she could and should have already filled in beforehand.

THUS I COULD READILY appreciate how the line behind us at the Sam's counter was becoming restless, and even hostile, as the conference on what to do continued. The cart contents of one gentleman consisted of a very large flat screen TV and a case of beer. I asked him if I could go home with him, but he refused to give me his address.

The store conferees came to the conclusion that the easiest way to get rid of me was to issue me a temporary free membership, so that I could pay for my purchases and disappear. The membership ended as soon as I forked over the cash. Perhaps the shortest membership of any kind in history.

"Stop!" I heard the clerk holler at me some 30 seconds after I'd made my escape. "Ohmygawd," I said to myself. "I thought I was in the clear, but obviously I must have paid with counterfeit bills or committed some other faux pas." I fortunately resisted the urge to run, because she was just returning my cell phone, which I had dropped during all the negotiations.

THE CONFEREES DECIDED the way to solve the Cobb part of the problem was for her to go to the service desk where they would issue her a duplicate personal card. However, the #1 computer refused to have anything to do with this fiasco, and refused to print the card. Thus she had to go to the second computer. It also wanted nothing to do with the whole mess, and again the card would not print.

By this time the comedy of errors had both customer and employees at the service counter in stitches, and all work had come to a halt.

Fortunately, the third computer was further away, and not having heard what was going on, printed out the new card. So now she was able to pay for her purchases by check. However the total appeared to be somewhat high. The reason being that the two chickens she had purchased had been billed at $9,415.56.

By this time, the aforementioned Mrs. Cobb had them so confused that they forgot she was the one responsible for the whole fiasco, and gave her a free umbrella as an apology.

Or perhaps what the gift meant was that it would be a rainy day in hell before she's welcome back in the store.

Sad News for the Ladies: What's Her Name Got Him

August 2008

I must hasten to explain that I did not compose the headlines for these columns when they ran in the Rome News-Tribune*!! Most were done by the very talented Pierre Noth when he was the editorial page editor. Just wanted to make sure you didn't think I was the one who thought my marriage was "sad news for the ladies."*

ALEX HAWKINS, WHO USED to play for the Atlanta Falcons, was noted for his late night carousing. One night when he arrived home at 7:00 AM, his wife demanded, "Where have you been all night?"

"I got home at 11:30 last night," he replied, trying as best he could to make his inebriated brain come up with a good excuse. "You had gone to bed, and I had forgotten my key. I didn't want to wake you, so I spent the night sleeping in the hammock in the backyard."

"We don't have a hammock in the backyard. We took it down three weeks ago."

"Nevertheless," said the plastered Hawkins with great dignity, "that's my story and I'm stickin' to it!"

"YOU LOOK LIKE MY second husband," the lady told me.

"Indeed?" I replied. "How many times have you been married?"

"Just once," said she. And that was the beginning of how I happen to have become engaged. Like Hawkins, that's my story and I'm stickin' to it.

Lord knows it's not something I really had planned to do. I was not like the husband who was asked by his wife, "If I should die first, would you remarry?"

"Of course not! Well, maybe after 10 years or more of loneliness if I found someone as lonely as I, I might possibly get married just for companionship."

"Would you let her live in my house?"

"Again, I have no plans to remarry! But on the off chance that I do way off in the future, I guess we might stay in your house if we could find no other place to live."

"Would you let her use my golf clubs?" she persisted.

"No. She couldn't do that. She's left handed."

You may have noted that I used no name in referring to my betrothed. The reason for this is that she has threatened me with severe bodily harm should I ever again mention her name in this column. Thus, coward that I am, I shall hereinafter refer to her only as "What's Her Name."

THE DISAPPOINTING THING THAT I have discovered from this experience, is that male solidarity and bonding, like the old gray mare, just ain't what it used to be. Years ago, if a husband stayed out all night, and told his wife he had been at a friend's house, his friends would have stood by him. If his wife was suspicious and called ten of his friends to see if he had stayed the night there, all ten would have sworn that he had indeed spent the night at his house. Approximately three would have maintained that furthermore he was still there.

But I have discovered that males no longer stick up for other men. This is demonstrated by the comments many of my friends(?) have made when they heard of my engagement. Examples:

Charlie Davidson: "Where did you find a blind woman?"

Bobby Kane: "You'd better get hitched in a hurry before she comes to her senses."

Gardner Wright: "I'm thrilled for you, but NOT for her!"

Floyd Roebuck: "She could have done much better than you!" Which seemed rather unkind and unchristian from a man of the cloth. Probably because, as a Baptist, he didn't know any better.

Bub Wilcox: "There's a long list of guys she could have done better with!"

"I agree," I told him. "However, I have perused that list, and find that your name is not upon it." This was payback for what he did to me a few years ago:

We had finished a round of golf, and he told me he had to rush home for his birthday party.

"I'm rather hurt that I am not invited," I told him.

"We had a long list of friends I wanted to invite, but we just didn't have room for everyone. However, your name was not even on that long list."

PIERRE NOTH: "Obviously, she is a former optometric patient of yours, and thus can't see what you look like." That also seemed a little non-supportive from my very own editor for these pieces.

Mike McDougald, speaking to What's Her Name:

"You poor thing."

Jim Clark, when he discovered What's Her Name's name: "She is a lovely and sweet lady."

Dave McCorkle: "How did she get hooked up with Runninger then?"

Clark: "My thoughts exactly."

Joel Todino: "Do you want me to be your best man? I may not be best, but I may be the only one you can find who will agree to stand up for you."

Ed Edmondson: "Please give her my condolences."

EVEN SOME FEMALES were a little ugly in their reactions.

Shelley Ballou, my ten year old granddaughter: When in a rare moment of humility, I told some family members that I had been told by many that What's Her Name might be too good for me, my own granddaughter, having become captivated by What's Her Name, responded with enthusiasm, "I agree!"

Flo Ansley: "Did you remember to ask her parents for permission?"

Ruth Martin: "Congratulations," said she, to me. Then she turned to What's Her Name and exclaimed, "Have you lost your mind?!"

THE ODD THING IS THAT What's Her Name and I are very much opposites. For example, she has a much more agreeable disposition than do I. That's why I was a little surprised and hurt when I told her I expected a hot breakfast every morning after we were married, and she replied, "That's no problem. All you have to do is put your cold cereal in the microwave for a few seconds." (This is also a big fat lie. I borrowed the story from Jim Rogers, who maintains that's what happened to him before he got married.)

About the only thing we do agree on, is that I'm adorable.

ANYWAY, I AM BEGINNING to lose all self confidence and sense of self worth with all these adverse comments.

One Plus One Is a Subtraction Problem

January 2009

"My wooden leg pained me somethin' fierce last night," cuzzin George told his buddy.

"There ain't no way a wooden leg can hurt!" sez his buddy Ezra.

"There is if yo' wife hits you over the head with it!"

It didn't get this bad. But after a couple of months of marriage, I discover I'm no longer the King of the Castle.

AS YOU MAY HAVE HEARD, What's Her Name, (hereinafter referred to as WHN), and I got hitched recently. The reason for the WHN alias is I have again been threatened with severe bodily harm by the lady, if I ever again write about her in this column. Hopefully this is due to shyness rather than a reluctance to have her name publicly associated with mine.

Taking connubial vows has necessitated my eating some of the words I expressed in other columns, wherein I recounted the benefits of being King of the Castle, living alone. For example, the advantages of being able to leave the cereal box on the kitchen table. I figured I was in trouble when I asked WHN if it was okay to continue to do so after we were married.

"Of course!" she enthusiastically replied. I was of course very pleased until she added, "As long as you paint it to match the décor of the kitchen."

I MUST CONFESS I STILL do not understand women, even after living for many moons with 2 wives (not simultaneously), 3 daughters, and 4 granddaughters. Although it appears that the weaker (ha!) sex craves time and labor saving devices, such as dishwashers, clothes dryers, microwaves, etc, they never seem to appreciate my simple time saving suggestions.

Leaving the cereal box on the table creates such a time and labor saving method. According to my calculations, it takes about 30 seconds to return the box to the cupboard after breakfast, and then another 30 seconds to bring it back to the table the next day. If my addition is correct, that is one minute per day.

Over the three years I lived alone, I figure I therefore have saved over one thousand minutes, or 18 hours of my valuable productive time. A similar time savings can be computed for taking dishes from the dishwasher only when needed, rather than the extra step of first placing them in the cupboard. I have yet to find a single female who appreciates these two time saving systems.

IN ADDITION, I HAVE DISCOVERED another advantage of leaving things on the table rather than putting them up. Ms. Neatnick (WHN), also decided the vitamin bottle should be removed from the table between meals. Which she proceeded to do. Now we can't find it, creating a monetary loss in addition to the time loss.

I also discover another financial disadvantage of becoming engaged and then married. My water bill has increased drastically, since I must shower and shave more frequently.

I MUST ADMIT THAT my fashion sense may not be of

the highest order. For example, I was once asked the color of the bedroom walls in my abode, and I had to admit that I didn't know. However there were extenuating circumstances. I had only lived here for 9 months at the time, plus the lights were off 99% of the time I spent in the bedroom. Thus in matters of taste, I must bow to the superior skill of WHN. After all, she has proven her discerning taste by her choice of mate.

Also I discover I must again be more careful of what I say. So that I don't goof up like the husband who complained to his wife after she had purchased $90 worth of cosmetics after they had agreed to economize.

"I bought them to make myself more beautiful for you," she tearfully explained. "Besides, you just bought a case of beer. Why did you do that?"

"Same reason," he unfortunately replied.

I MUST MAKE MENTION of the posh engagement party given us by her classy, sophisticated friends, Ginger Grant, Penny Mitchell, and Virginia Bellew. It was a swank champagne yacht cruise on the beautiful and romantic Little River, in the lovely state of Alabama. As we cruised along (actually the yacht turned out to be a pontoon boat), seated among the gorgeous artificial flowers, we were served champagne in exquisite fluted glasses. The plastic wasn't even chipped or cracked in some of them!

I was also pleasantly surprised to hear WHN say that by nature, she is a forgiving person. That sounded as if I might get away with things, without being nagged. I decided to test my premise by asking her, "After the nuptials, would you forgive me if I ran around with another woman?"

"Of course," she replied. "I'd miss you too."

"WHY?" YOU MAY ASK, "have you reentered the matrimonial state in spite of all these adverse factors?"

Two reasons:

1. She laughs at my jokes.
2. In the game of life, the love card trumps all other cards.

Silly Jokes, Whimsical Pranks, Part of Dr. Jim Kelley's Legacy

March, 2009

The late Dr. Jim Kelley was a master story teller and prankster. He delighted in making females often the recipient of such. This column I wrote following his demise gives some examples.

"Luigi, why you wanna marry Rosita?" asked his friend Pasquale. "She'sa slept with every man in our village."

"I know," replied Luigi. "But itsa only a small village."

This is the kind of stupid story my friend Dr. Jim Kelley, used to tell. But the way he delivered them made them hilarious even when they weren't all that funny. I'll miss them, AND him, since his death.

"I HAVE ALWAYS believed that his patients got well faster because of his optimistic outlook for them and for the world around him. He'll make a great angel," David Harvey told me.

I agree. But first the other angels are going to have to get used to disruptions he and his jokes will cause. When thunder and lightening, and power outages, took place during his funeral, I couldn't help but think, "Well, he's arrived."

"Had Jim and Bub Wilcox ever decided to quit doctoring and gone on the road as a pair of comedians, they would have played to standing room crowds," was Dr. Bill Allen's comment. "Many times, they had those of us in the surgeon's lounge roaring and wiping tears. Unfortunately, most of those stories could never be printed in a family newspaper."

THAT'S THE PROBLEM I HAD, finding some of his stories that would pass censorship, to include in this column. I'll have to pass over his "Propitious moment" story, and also his "hindlick maneuver" story, but will report one he enjoyed telling, and told so well, particularly with his marvelous foreign accent:

"Rosa fell out of the choir loft in an Italian church one Sunday. Fortunately her feet caught in a chandelier to break her fall, but suspended upside down her robe and dress dropped down around her neck, leaving her body exposed. 'Anyone whosa look at Rosa, God's a-gonna strike blind,' announced the priest in trying to alleviate the situation. All of the parishioners immediately dropped their eyes.

"After a few moments, Pasquale whispered to his friend Luigi, 'I think I'm a-gonna risk one eye.'"

IT WASN'T ONLY THE JOKES that made Jim such a joy to be around. The things he did were often also humorous:

"I was walking through the lobby of Floyd Hospital one day a number of years ago," Anne Culpepper told me. "Jim walked up behind me and without saying a word, took me by the elbow and steered me to the reception desk.

"'Get a nurse down here and tell her to give this woman an enema as soon as possible' he told the receptionist. Then without another word, he walked off, leaving me with the large number of people in the reception area looking at me in a very strange way."

And there's no telling how many times his wife Eva had to listen to him introduce her as his "first wife." "Keeps her on her toes," he always explained.

IN ADDITION, JIM'S GREAT sense of humor also made him enjoy jokes that were told at his expense. To get even with him for something he had done to me, I used his name in a story in an article I wrote for a national optometric journal many years ago, which he enjoyed remembering to me for many years. Since the article was about occupational back problems, as my intro in the article I used the following story:

"When I had an appointment with Dr. Jim Kelley about my leg problems, he told me that he'd have me walking in six weeks," a friend told me.

"Did he succeed?" I asked.

"He sure did! He charged me so much I had to sell my car."

HE'LL BE MISSED BY ALL, but he leaves a great legacy on how to live an enjoyable and satisfying life. He concentrated on his blessings, rather than his problems. Because of his positive attitude and sense of humor, everyone thoroughly enjoyed his company! Even when he was in bad health, he never complained, and kept his pleasant demeanor.

I've known some folks who act like they think they're big wheels, but are really no more than a hubcap. He was the opposite, a big wheel with many outstanding honors and accomplishments, and a reputation for being an outstanding surgeon. Yet he never was a stuffed shirt about it---he was always plain old Jim.

HE WOULD NEVER FORGIVE me if I closed this column on such a serious note, so I'll close with another story that he liked, when someone told it on him.

"Did the surgery go okay?" a patient of his, upon whom he had just operated, was asked.

"Well, I didn't much like the four letter word he used during the surgery!"

"That's inexcusable. What was the word?"

"Oops."

Fashion, Decor Changed Since Wedding

May, 2009

"When we got married, I told you I'd carry you over the rough places of life, didn't I?" said the husband. "That's right. And you ain't missed a single one of them, either!"

I discover after a few months of marriage, that when you get hitched during your senior years, you are both pretty well set in your ways. It takes some getting used to. (But it's worth it.)

SINCE WRITING A RECENT COLUMN on the life changes involved with having remarried after three years of being a widower, some folks have asked if I'm adapting to these changes any better with the passage of time.

I guess the answer has to be "yes", since I remain happy and content in my marital relationship with What's Her Name (WHN), despite the fact that we have little in common. For example:

I am pretty much a devotee of the McCorkle School of Fashion. "The nice thing about wearing a turtle neck shirt," said its founder, learned educator, Dr. David McCorkle, (kiddingly I hope), "is that if you spill something major on it, you can turn it around backwards, and again have a relatively clean shirt front."

While WHN can see and disapprove a tiny shirt front stain at 95 paces, that I can't find even with a microscope.

FASHIONWISE IT APPEARS to me that women's definition of something that is old and out of fashion is anything that was purchased prior to a week ago Thursday. While the male criterium of whether wearing apparel is new and fashionable, is whether it was purchased subsequent to October of 1982.

Other differences I find include the towels and washcloths in my abode now always match. However I have noted that they don't get me any cleaner or dryer than the mismatches I was formerly using.

"Haven't you noticed how the new living room drapes pull the room together?" WHN asked me. Hell, I hadn't even noticed that it was falling apart.

And our opinion of whether the house is clean is vastly different. As Dave Barry once said, "The primary difference between men and women is that women can see extremely small quantities of dirt, even at the molecule level. Men don't notice it until it forms clumps large enough to support agriculture."

ANOTHER ADAPTATION I'VE HAD to make is the role reversal. In my previous marriage, I was the one who worked, and my wife did not. But now, WHN is still working while I am retired. Thus I am now the one who fixes breakfast while wearing a dirty robe with hair up in curlers, while she gets ready for work.

"Why would such a lovely lady with a good job marry an old goat like you?" you may ask. I could be wrong, but I like to think that the reason is explained by the old story of the laundress who worked 12 hours a day in order to support her good for nothing husband who did nothing.

"I MAKES THE LIVING," she explained, "but he makes the living worthwhile."

I do try to be supportive. I always insist that she rest for a few minutes after returning home from work, before she fixes dinner and cleans up the kitchen.

BUT DESPITE OUR DIFFERENCES, I think I may have found the secret to a perfect marriage. I think perhaps the reason our marriage is so successful is that with my lousy hearing, and WHN's soft voice, I can't hear a durned thing she says. And when I do occasionally hear her, with my Yankee upbringing and her Savannah Magnolia accent, I usually have no idea as to what she's saying.

For example I still have not been able to differentiate what she means by the word "Ahm." I never can tell if she is referring to the thing her hand is attached to, or if she's stating an intent. (Ah'm fixin' to go.) Her alphabet consists of only 25 letters, since the letter "R" is superfluous in her vocabulary.

We have thought of converting to sign language to communicate better. Only problem there is that my entire repertoire of sign language consists of the "signs" for only two words, "boring", and "b.s." Somehow I do not believe it would be very healthy to use either in responding to anything she says.

Come to think of it, WHN and I do have one thing in common. We were married on the same day.

Treat Hearing Loss with a Bit of Humor

September, 2009

In which I discover that the hearing loss that often accompanies getting older can cause complications in communicating with a wife.

"PLEASE PRAY FOR my hearing!" a mean-looking gentleman requested of the evangelist at the revival.

"Heal!" shouted the evangelist, as he looked toward heaven, and smote the petitioner on both ears. Then turning toward him, he asked, "How's your hearing now?"

"I don't know yet. It doesn't take place until next Monday at the courthouse."

All by way of introducing "hearing" as the subject of today's treatise. However, not the courthouse kind, but instead what people do via the skin and gristle doohickies on each side of their heads.

HAVING OVER THE YEARS gradually lost much of my hearing ability, I find that the best way to endure it is to treat it with a sense of humor. It's the only way to come to terms with society's tendency to interpret the hearing impaired's miscomprehension as being caused by stupidity rather than poor hearing.

Before I retired, a sweet little old lady patient of mine demonstrated this facility. When I asked her during case history if she had any health problems, she replied, "Yes, I have Aids." Then she laughed as she saw my expression of disbelief and confusion, and continued, "One in each ear."

THERE ARE A NUMBER of problems involved with hearing loss. One is the misunderstanding of questions asked. As an example, we used to tell the story on the late John Read about him telling me of the marvelous new hearing aid he had purchased. "It cost a lot but it's worth it," he reported. "My hearing is completely restored.

"That's great," I told him. "What kind is it?"

"It's a quarter to three," he replied as he looked at his watch.

Or the elderly hard of hearing lady who was undergoing a physical exam. "Big breaths," said the physician as he placed the stethoscope on her chest.

"Yes," she sighed. "But you should have seen them 40 years ago."

I can relate to the three hearing impaired Englishman driving through the countryside, when they came to a small village. "Is this Wembley?" asked one.

"No, I think it's Thursday," replied another.

"So am I!" said the third. "Let's stop at that Pub up the street."

EVEN MORE DANGEROUS IS THE misunderstanding of instructions. An elderly man was walking jauntily down the street with a young peroxide blonde on his arm, when he ran into his cardiologist, Dr. Frank Stegall.

"What do you think you're doing?" asked Frank.

"Just following your instructions," replied the gentleman. "You told me to be cheerful and get a hot momma."

"No, no, no! What I told you was, 'be careful, you've got a heart murmur.'"

ANOTHER PROBLEM is the difficulty of keeping up with hearing aids, since they are so small and easily misplaced. And expensive! George Home once told me of a gentleman undergoing an ear exam.

"Why do you have a suppository in your ear?" asked the MD.

"Thank God," replied the gentleman. "Now I know where I lost my hearing aid."

HARD OF HEARING FOLKS are often hesitant to admit it, and blame the problem on others. One gentleman was convinced that his wife's hearing, rather than his own, was the problem in their difficult communication. To test it out, while she was working at the sink, he stood about 20 feet behind her, and asked softly, "What's for dinner?" When he got no response, he moved in to 10 feet, and softly repeated the question. Still no response, and he figured this proved her loss of hearing.

But just to be certain, he moved in to five feet, and again repeated the question. She turned to him and said in a loud voice, "I've already told you twice we're having chicken."

UNFORTUNATELY, WHN has perfect hearing. She can hear a pin drop 90 feet away. This is hard to live with. I was two rooms removed from her, talking on the phone, and in a soft voice told the person something I didn't want WHN to hear. Unfortunately, she heard every word.

However, my hearing difficulty does have some domestic advantages. When I don't respond to some of her questions or directions, I can always plead that I didn't hear them. And when she requests that I do certain household duties, I can always pretend I don't hear, and perhaps she'll give up and do them herself. (This, however, rarely works.)

"WE need to take out the garbage," she says. This always reminds me of the time the Lone Ranger and Tonto were surrounded by 1,000 Indians. "We're in trouble," said the Lone Ranger. "Woddya mean 'We', White Boy?" responded Tonto.

I thought maybe I could cure her of this "we means you" bit. So the last time she said, "We need to take out the garbage," I picked up the garbage in one hand, and with the other hand pulled her along with me to the garbage can, so that indeed "we" did take out the garbage.

Reportedly, some people don't mind losing their hearing.

"Mr. Jones, you're going to have to quit drinking," Dr. Toby Morgan told a patient, "or you're going to lose your hearing."

"That's okay, Doc," replied Mr. Jones. "What I've been drinkin' is a whole lot better than what I've been hearin'!"

I'LL CLOSE THIS EPISTLE with some words of advice on how you folks with good hearing can best adapt to your increasingly older, and thus deafer, compatriots, such as I.

1. Please realize that the hearing impaired's miscomprehension of what's going on is probably due not to stupidity, but rather to not being able to hear most of what's being discussed.
2. When a hard of hearing person sits next

to you at a play, a movie, a board meeting, etc., run, don't walk, to a different seat. It will save you from an evening of responding repeatedly to "Woddidhesay?"

Practical Jokes and Dirty Tricks Explained

December 2009

Although this one is mostly not about the female species, I had to include it just so you can read the delightful tale Sam Levenson tells about the resourcefulness of mothers.

As a completely useless service to humanity, I have completed a research study to classify the various types of dirty tricks and practical jokes:

PURPOSEFUL—Some dirty tricks are necessary because they serve a purpose. To illustrate: the following story told by the late comedian Sam Levenson, whose humor I adored.

"My mother was very resourceful," said Levenson. "One day when I was a kid, relatives dropped in to visit right at suppertime. 'I'm going to invite the relatives to stay for supper, so there won't be enough chicken to go around,' Momma told all us boys. 'So when the plate is passed, I want you all to say that you don't want any chicken.'

"Even though we were all starved, we dutifully refused to take any chicken when the platter was passed. When everyone had finished supper, Momma announced, 'We have pie for dessert. But all you boys who didn't eat your chicken don't get any dessert.'"

BRAGGER PUT DOWN—There are some folks who like to brag about their possessions. It's fun to put them down. The late Bill Maynard told me about the man in Atlanta he knew who had a Volkswagen. He boasted continually about his good gas mileage. (Which reminds me of the old Chrysler Imperial I once had that got 20 miles to the gallon. Eight in town and twelve on the road.)

His neighbor got tired of hearing him brag, and decided he'd give him something to really brag about. Early every morning he'd sneak into the neighbor's garage and add a half gallon of gas to to the Volkswagen's tank.

Now the neighbor was bragging about getting more than 50 miles to the gallon. After two weeks of this, the neighbor began siphoning out a half gallon each morning. The bragger drove himself and his mechanic crazy trying to determine why he suddenly was getting only twelve miles to the gallon.

Even wives get tired of the boasting. "This card says I am a leader of men and irresistable to women!" bragged a man as he stepped down from a scale that gave weight and fortune.

"It got your weight wrong, too," said his wife as she read the card.

WHEELER-DEALER PUT DOWN—Some folks like to brag about what great wheeler-dealers they are. They can be bested with by the high or low estimate system.

"I bought this oriental rug four years ago for just $1.200," they tell you. "Guess how much it's worth now." They, of course, want you to make a low estimate, like $1,500. Then they can triumphantly say, "Nope, it's quadrupled in value. Worth almost five big ones now!"

Instead, you purposely way overestimate, and say innocently, "Gee, I don't know. $100,000?" This takes the wind out of their sails, and they will no longer bother you with stories of their business acumen.

A second example: "My new car lists for $32,000. Guess how much I paid for it after dickering with the salesman?"

"Gee, I don't know," you again say innocently. "$15,000?"

INSTANTANEOUS—These are the practical jokes that are successfully designed and executed on the spur of the moment.

Many years ago, a stray cat took up residence at a house in Lindale. The cat was always underfoot and a real nuisance. Finally one day the homeowner captured the cat, put it in his car, and drove 25 miles into the country to get rid of it.

However, his neighbor saw him do it, and realized what he was doing. So he got in his car and followed him the 25 miles. After the man dropped off the cat, he continued up the road a ways to turn around. Meanwhile, the neighbor picked up the cat, turned around, and drove rapidly back to town to arrive with the cat before the man returned.

When the gentleman arrived back home a couple of minutes later, he found the cat sitting on the porch waiting for him. I wish I could have seen the expression on that man's face.

Surviving a Recent Cold Spell

January, 2010

Why is it that wives feel they must awaken their husbands in the middle of the night, to share with them the news that they heard a strange noise?

"JOHNNY, HOW DO YOU spell 'weather?'" said the teacher.

"'W-A-T-H-O-U-R,'" replied Johhny.

"My goodness," said the teacher. "That's the worst spell of weather we've had in a long time."

We also recently have had a bad spell of weather, with the temperature not even getting up to the freezing point for a few days. I was fervently praying that we not have any furnace problems during that spell. But, sure enough, one night about 4:00 AM, our furnace began making odd vibration noises.

WITH MY LOUSY HEARING, I wouldn't have heard or known about it, and gone on sleeping blissfully. However, What's Her Name unfortunately has extremely acute hearing, and the noise woke her up.

Like all wives, she loves to share such events with her husband, so shook me awake to tell me the furnace was making a noise. I thanked her profusely for awakening me to impart this fascinating bit of information.

"What's causing the noise?" she asked me.

"How in (blazes) should I know?" was my tender response.

ALDOUS HUXLEY ONCE SAID the secret of life can be summed up in just five words, "You get used to it." My philosophy of life is instead, "If you ignore problems, they may go away."

"A pine cone has probably dropped in the fan on the tower outdoors," I told WHN, "and is causing the vibration," was the only feeble (and stupid) reasoning I could come up with in order to hopefully get her to cease worrying about it, so I could go back to sleep.

Fortunately the noise stopped, and I was able to return to slumberland. Until about 30 minutes later when I was again awakened by her, as she said accusingly:

"We don't have any pine trees or pine cones in our yard!"

When finally the roads de-iced sufficiently for WHN to drive to work, I told her to please drive carefully. She seemed to genuinely appreciate my concern for her safety until I screwed the whole thing up by continuing:

"I don't want you sliding into anything and putting dents in the car."

"No supper for you tonight," was her rejoinder.

ANYWAY, THE FRIGID WEATHER reminded me of how lucky most of us are to have efficient furnaces. The "good old days" weren't all that great when it came to getting heat. When I was a small boy back in the 1930's, we would spend Christmas in Huntington, Indiana with my grandparents. Their modern, at the time, house was heated by a pot bellied coal stove in the living room and a wood cooking stove in the kitchen.

The upstairs had no heating at all, and that's where

I had to sleep, with temperatures down around zero. Seven or eight blankets made it bearable at night, but I can still remember the pain of getting out of bed in the morning with the temperature near zero outside, and not much warmer inside.

While flipping through the channels with the remote, on one of our cold evenings, I saw a preacher talking about the fires of hell. He should have waited until summer to preach on this theme. Right then, with the temperature 15 degrees outside, those fires sounded right comforting to me!

Memories of Momma

February, 2010

My mother (and father) had different ideas as to what was "good for me" than did I.

I FIND I AM SUSPICIOUS of anything that is presented to me as being "good for me." It's probable that childhood experiences have ingrained this phobia in me. Back then I could always tell something was going to happen that I wasn't going to like, when my parents told me, "It's good for you."

Comedian Alan King told of a conversation at the dinner table when he was a child:

"Eat your vegetables," said his father.

"Why?" asked Alan.

"Because they're good for you."

"Why are they good for me?"

"Because I'm gonna swat you across the head if you don't eat them—that's why they're good for you!"

This logic was probably as good or better than my parents'. They had not the benefit of today's nutritional and vitamin research, to determine what was good for me. They didn't need it.

They had a very simple method of determining the nutritional value of any food, namely that if it tasted bad and I didn't like it, then it was good for me.

THE SAME PRINCIPLE APPLIED to medicines. The worse it tasted the more miraculous its curative powers. (Remember castor oil?) In addition the more it cost, the better it was for you.

One of the most difficult things in life is trying to shove a spoonful of medicine into the gullet of an unwilling child. That's what my father was attempting one day with my sobbing four year old brother. After three spoonfuls had been deposited on his shirt, my old man began to lose his temper.

"This medicine cost a lot of money, and you're going to take it!" he thundered. Finally he was able hold his son's nose, and when he opened his mouth to breathe, was able to thrust a spoonful down his throat. He began to gag, and tearfully said to our father, "If we can afford it, I think I'm going to throw up." (true story)

SINCE MY CHILDHOOD occurred during the Depression of the 1930's when money was scarce, my parents had a corollary maxim regarding food: If it's cheap and plentiful, it's also good for you.

My mother had a vegetable garden every summer. The Jolly Green Giant she was not. Every year we'd get a few woody radishes, a few ears of tough corn, and a whole lot of weeds. Her one triumph every year was green beans. The woman was a world class expert when it came to green beans. Every year she produced a bumper crop, and I do mean bumper!

For 5-6 weeks every summer we ate them at EVERY meal, until they were coming out our ears. The highlight of my summers was when the last green bean had been consumed.

My mother's other food theory was to feed the most

fattening, and therefore tastiest, food to the scrawniest child. In those days, milk was not homogenized, and the cream rose to the top. Our youngest brother was skinny, so he was given the cream off the top, while my other brother and I drank the remaining skim milk.

I'll have to admit, however, that their theory worked. My middle brother weighed about 170 pounds when he passed away, and I weigh in at 180. Baby brother has maintained a weight of 260 for many years.

ALSO "GOOD FOR ME" was my mother's decision that I should take ballroom dancing lessons when I was about 12 years old, so that I could attain the social graces. Doing something this sissy, I hated with a purple passion.

Anyway, these childhood experiences are the reason I become suspicious about anything that's "good for me."

Women Patients Say Some of the Craziest Things

May, 2010

I've discovered that lots of sweet little old ladies are instead right feisty. Like the one who was stopped by a state trooper who asked her, "Do you have a gun permit for that revolver in the passenger seat?" "Sure do. Also for the one in the glove compartment and for one in my purse."

"Just what are you so afraid of?" he asked her.

"Not a damned thing!" was her emphatic reply.

While I was still practicing optometry, I (and other health care practitioners) discovered some female patients will also come up with such strange responses.

"YOUR CHECK CAME BACK, Mrs. Jones," complained the doctor.

"So did my arthritis!" she replied.

Doctor/patient relations are the source of many humorous stories. Even puns:

"I want you to chew and swallow a half inch of this leather thong every day," said the medicine man to the Indian chief. "It'll cure your illness."

"I'm still sick," the chief told the medicine man when he returned the following week. "The thong is ended, but the malady lingers on."

Most such stories are, of course, contrived. But in addition I am told of many strange and humorous happenings in doctor's offices that are true.

"WHILE ON A MISSION trip to Jamaica, a lady on our team was assisting a Jamaican gentleman with his new glasses," an optometrist in Perry, GA emailed me. "After she had finished adjusting them, in his strong Jamaican dialect he said, 'May I have a keese?'

"Unfamiliar with local customs, she obliged him with a kiss on the cheek. The startled gentleman promptly clarified his request. 'No, no! I would like to have a keese to keep my glasses in.'"

"HOW'S YOUR HEALTH?" I once asked a patient during case history.

"I'm getting old, Doc, and can't do things like I used to. My wife calls our water bed, 'The Dead Sea.'"

"I've gained too much weight," another patient answered when I asked her the same question. "When I step on my talking scales, it tells me to come back alone."

MY GOOD FRIEND, VETERINARIAN Dr. Conney Batson, tells of an experience he had many years ago. A poor widow living in the country phoned him to ask if he would come examine her cow. Which he did.

"How much do I owe you?" she inquired.

"Not anything," he replied, knowing that the poor lady was almost destitute.

"I insist on paying," she answered.

"Okay, you owe me one dollar," he told her.

"That's better," she said. " Just send me a bill."

ANOTHER PURPORTEDLY TRUE story I heard was about the lady who saw her medical records on a desk while waiting to see the doctor, who specialized in pulmonary/breathing problems. She was infuriated when she saw the initials S.O.B. written on the top page.

"If that's what he thinks of me, I'll never come back here again," she stormed at the nurse as she walked out.

She sheepishly returned to the exam room when the nurse explained to her that S.O.B. stood for "Shortness of Breath."

A New Jersey optometrist told me of an "Abbot and Costello" routine he had with a patient:

"Please read the top line on the chart," he told her.

"Do you want me to read the letters with both eyes?" she asked.

"Right."

"Do you want me to read it with my right eye first?"

"No, I'd like for you to read it with both eyes."

"Okay, which eye should I begin with?"

BEFORE I RETIRED FROM optometric practice, I heard many strange stories about how patients had found a contact lens after losing it. One of the oddest came to me from a Wisconsin optometrist:

"I had dispensed a pair of contact lenses to a teen age girl who lives in the country," he wrote. "A few days later, she put the lenses on the top of the toilet tank. While flushing she accidentally knocked the lenses into the commode, and they also flushed down the toilet.

"Her father owned the local septic tank cleaning business, so he pumped the septic tank, and sprayed the contents on the back 40 acres. He then made all the family don rubber boots and gloves, and peruse the area to search for the lenses. And they found them!"

If it had been me, I do believe I'd just as soon the lenses would have stayed lost.

Discovering New Things about Your Wife

July, 2010

"Ain't you ashamed to have yore wife support you by takin' in laundry?" (Again from Boogar Hollow.)

Uncle Ned sez, "I sure am! But she's too ignorant to do anything else."

Dr. Milder was also brave with this poem.

MY FRIEND DR. BEN MILDER of St. Louis, wrote a humorous poem in his book, *The Good Book Also Says,* on having second thoughts about being married. Interestingly, every line rhymes with every other line:

Before the minister intoned, "Let no man put asunder,"
I should have had some second thoughts, and possibly have shunned her.
She's like the buccaneers of old, whose only goal was plunder.
I'm on the brink of destitution, struggling to fund her.
And now, besieged by all the bill collectors who have dunned her,
It finally has dawned on me, just like a clap of thunder,
That my banker has been saying, "It looks like

you're going under."
And now to make things even worse, she has become rotunder.
So when that clergyman intoned, "Let no man put asunder,"
And I agreed, could it have been a monumental blunder?
I wonder!

For reasons of maintaining my physical health, I must hasten to say the poem does not state my views—I did NOT make a blunder in marrying What's Her Name a couple of years ago. I'm thankful every day (well, almost every day) that I did so. But I must admit I have found that after you've been married awhile, you do keep discovering things about your mate that you didn't know before you got hitched."

1. She has a brown rather than green thumb. We have possibly the largest tomato plant in the city of Rome. Only problem is that it has no tomatoes on it. Another example—one of the prizes she received when she was selected Older Worker of the Year for northwest Georgia, was a tulip bulb. She planted it in a pot and nursed it tenderly until it came up. It had to be one of the worst looking flowers ever known to mankind. It was a drab color and the first tulip I've ever seen that was dried up, shrunken, and wrinkled from the start.

I couldn't resist. I decided to enter it in the Garden Club's flower show. I must apologize to the nice ladies running the show, for the disruption I caused. I think they thought I was serious and explained to me kindly that I had to be a member to make an entry. Even when I offered to join, I was still rebuffed.

So I placed the tulip next to a blue ribbon I took from another entry, and took a picture of it to give to WHN. However she did not seem to appreciate my thoughtfulness.

2. She doesn't realize that neatness is actually a function of time, not sloppiness. If I leave dishes in the sink, WHN assumes I am being messy and leaving them there for to take care of. Not true! I'll put them in the dishwasher as soon as I notice them, or as soon as they bother me.

Unfortunately, some things don't bother me right away. Such as dirty clothes on the floor, a cereal box on the table, dishes in the sink, etc. I'm really just as neat as WHN, it's just that she gets bothered sooner. Does this mean I am a slob? I think not. I just have a slower reaction time in noticing disorder than does she.

"When I discovered how much it bugged my wife when I left my underwear on the living room floor," reported another thoughtful and considerate husband, "I took it off in the kitchen instead."

3. She is thoughtful about boasting about her great grandchildren. She is not like the

lady who said, "Have I ever shown you the pictures of my grandchildren?"

"No, you haven't," said her companion. "And I certainly do appreciate it!!"

4. I didn't realize she would keep secrets from me. She came home the other day with a child's rocking chair, and some toys. It was quite a shock to discover that she is evidently planning on becoming pregnant, and our raising a family, without first discussing it with me.

To be continued next week. Unless WHN breaks my writing arm first.

What's Her Name Has Many Facets

August, 2010

I discover that senior marriages take some getting used to.

"ONE SATISFYING ASPECT of marriage," reported comedian Paul Reiser, "is attending your friends' weddings, and try not to fall on the floor laughing because they have no idea what married life will be like. Even so, weddings typically offer great entertainment value.

"I remember when my friend Jimmy got married," continued Reiser. "I was one of six groomsmen. We decided that we were going to convince him that he had a cliff hanger (something in his nose.) Jimmy came out and stood near the altar. As each of us walked down the aisle to join him, we'd point discreetly to our noses. Jimmy would pick at his nose, and then look over at us like, 'Did I get it?' We'd look back and silently mouth, 'Nah, you didn't get it.' He spent the entire wedding picking at his nose."

I hasten to assure WHN that I am not one of those men like Reiser, who take marriage lightly. I'm not at all like the sorry husband who told his wife, "If I die first, I want you to marry George."

"But I thought you hated George," she replied.

"I do!" he said fervently.

If you recall, last week's exciting episode was about

the new things men find about their wives after a couple of years of marriage. Further observations regarding things I've discovered about WHN:

SHE HAS AN INQUISITIVE AND IMAGINATIVE mind. While visiting friends in a Bloomington, Indiana retirement community, we discovered that right next to the commode was a pull cord mounted on the wall. I didn't have the guts to try it to see what it was for, but curiosity got the better of WHN. She decided since the name on the device was "Arial," it must be an air freshener. So she pulled the cord.

As it turned out, pulling the cord set off an alarm in the central office, and very shortly a man rushed to the house to discover what the emergency was. Our hosts explained what had happened, but did not want to embarrass WHN so did not tell her what she had done. So the next day, she decided to freshen the air again, and again pulled the cord. With the same result—a man from the central office rushing to see what the emergency was.

By that time, our friends decided to heck with any embarrassment it might cause, and asked her to please knock it off.

The whole episode reminded me of the story about a man who went in the Ladies Room, since the Men's Room was out of order. As he sat on the commode, he noticed a button on the wall, with the initials "TR" on it. Curiosity got the best of him, so he punched the button to see what would happen. He woke up six hours later in the hospital, in great pain.

"What happened?" he asked groggily of the nurse.

"The 'TR' on that button you pushed, stands for 'Tampax Remover'," she replied.

However I must admit I did something worse while there. A friend of my host had told me a naughty story, whose punch line consisted of a very bad word. While in a golf cart on the way to dinner, I told the story to the aforesaid host. We arrived at the dinner locale just as I was uttering the BAD word. I looked up and was horrified to see a lady standing about six feet away.

"Way to go!" said my friend. "That's my preacher's wife." Shortly thereafter, she said to him, "I haven't seen you in church lately." I guess she figured he needed it with crude friends such as I. After those two episodes, we are not expecting another invitation to visit them again any time soon.

1. She may not be as well-loved by her employees as I had thought. She told them kiddingly that she would retire as soon as I made a fortune selling the book I co-authored, *Fixing Stupid.*

   So help me, as soon as they heard this, every single one of them bought a book, some of them more than one.
2. She takes the joy out of being cantankerous. With my advancing years, I discovered how much I enjoyed the freedom to be crotchety, and no longer have to worry about being nice to folks. But WHN is so durned thoughtful and nice, I find myself instead feeling guilty and ashamed when I act curmudgeonly.

   She drives me crazy being so thoughtful not only to people, but also to animals.

For example, she read somewhere that birds like to use dryer lint in building their nests. So now whenever she cleans lint out of the dryer, instead of throwing it away, she takes it out to the backyard for the birdies to utilize.

3. She doesn't criticize. A man asked an American Indian what was his wife's name.

   "She called 'Five Horses'," the Indian replied.

   "That's an unusual name. What does it mean?"

   "Indian name. It mean "Nag, Nag, Nag, Nag, Nag."

I'm fortunate in discovering that WHN doesn't nag. However, this is probably because her husband is so perfect that she can find nothing to nag him about.

4. I've also discovered she has a marvelous sense of humor. And I do hope she keeps it while reading this epistle.

Why Do Women Treat Their Dogs Better Than Their Husbands?

September, 2010

"All you have to do for a dog is feed it and provide it with a place to live, and walk it every morning even when you're really tired and it's raining, and regularly take it to the veterinarian for shots and de-wormings and various other procedures that can run into the thousands of dollars," wrote humorist Dave Barry. "And in return you get an animal that really and truly and sincerely loves you, or anyone else who happens to feed it."

Nevertheless, it seems that most women are nicer to their dogs than they are to their husbands.

"HAVE YOU HEARD ABOUT the new Korean cookbook?" some joker asked me recently. "It's entitled *How To Wok Your Dog*." It does seem rather strange that dogs are part of the menu in some Asian countries, while here they are deified.

"Attacking dogs is more dangerous than attacking the efficacy of prayer," according to author H. Allen Smith in his book *Lost in the Horse Latitudes*. Nevertheless I feel constrained to make a few observations about dogs and their owners. Even though in the past I've discovered that while kidding women in these columns is usually received with good humor, doing so with dogs often is received with downright hostility.

PEOPLE ARE MORE PROTECTIVE of their dogs than they are of their spouses. "Like more than half the women in a recent survey, Kaye Nipper pampers her pets more than she does her spouse," wrote Marlon Manuel in a column for an Atlanta newspaper a few years ago.

"What's wrong with that?" said Nipper. "I have four dogs that are treated better than my husband." When asked why, she answered, "They don't talk back."

"SIDNEY WHIPPLE CAME BACK from a Christmas shopping expedition one day to tell of a small adventure he had in Saks Fifth Avenue," Smith also wrote. "He was waiting at the jewelry counter when up came a richly dressed woman with a tiny dog on a leash. Sidney, always amiable, bent down to pat the dog on the head. The dog snarled and tried to take off Mr. Whipple's finger.

"This was most embarrassing to the lady. She spoke a few words to her pet, employing the customary baby talk, then turned apologetically to Sidney. 'Don't you pay a *bit* of attention to him,' she said. 'He's just angry because I won't take him to the toy department.'"

This reminded me of the gentleman who saw a young boy walking up the street with a dog at his heels. "Does your dog bite?" asked the gentleman. When the boy said he did not, the man leaned over to pet the dog, who proceeded to take a chunk out of his hand.

"I thought you said your dog doesn't bite!"

"He don't," said the lad. "That ain't my dog."

"AN ANIMAL RESEARCH LABORATORY recently released 40 beagles for adoption after protests by movie star Kim Basinger," wrote Paul Mulshine in a newspaper article 10-12 years ago. "And when I saw the photos of those big-eyed beagles in the paper, I confess that I felt the same way Basinger felt when she told the media, 'I'm feeling very emotional about this.'"

"Me too. I'm feeling very emotional," continued Mulshine. "Not about the dogs though. About the neighbors of the people who will adopt them. Have you ever lived next door to a Beagle? They are one breed of which it can truly be said their bark is worse than their bite."

When I first came to Rome many moons ago, our house had no air conditioning. Thus it was necessary to keep the bedroom windows open at night to keep from sweltering. Two very nice dogs lived next door. The problem was that they slept all day, so that they could spend their nights barking just outside my open window. Complaining to the neighbor did no good. (It's usually not the dogs that cause the problems, it's the owners.)

"IT'S SO QUIET AND PEACEFUL here when we sit outside on our terrace," What's Her Name recently commented. "I guess it's because there aren't any dogs outdoors barking in this (retirement homes) community."

Quite an admission from WHN! She is one of the leading dog lovers of all time. Before we were married she owned and adored a sweet (but stupid) boxer named Grace. Since large outdoor dogs weren't permitted in my neighborhood, she had to choose between Grace and me.

"I never thought she'd choose you over Grace!" friend Penny Mitchell told me. But she did. I think what turned the trick in my favor was that she realized that being smarter than Grace, I could be trained to take out the garbage. People who maintain that dogs are highly intelligent never met Grace. She was usually tranquil, but whenever she got loose she would always get into a fight with another dog. It was never a Pekinese, but always a Great Dane twice her size.

WHN had spent a small fortune in tuition sending her to doggy school. She never quite graduated—in fact evidently never passed a single course.

"She's a beautiful and lovable dog, but when you look into her eyes," said WHN's son Tom Cobb, the present owner of Grace, "you realize there ain't nothing behind them."

IT OCCURS TO ME HOWEVER that perhaps dogs really are smarter than humans. They're the ones who get free room and board without having to do a lick of work. Another proof is that you rarely see dogs humiliating themselves by following humans with a pooper scooper in their paws.

When Legend Becomes Fact

November, 2010

I had to include this one because one of the stories illustrates that trustworthy as are we husbands, sometimes wives seem to get suspicious. The last "legend" herein describes how women often are not exactly expert when it comes to automobiles.

A HUSBAND AND WIFE WERE invited to a Halloween costume party, and the wife rented costumes for both of them. But on the night of the party, she had a headache and felt too ill to attend. So her husband put on his costume and went without her.

But about 9:00, she felt better and decided to attend the party after all. Since her husband hadn't seen her costume, she decided to remain incognito, in order to see how he behaves in her absence. When she arrived at the party, she spotted him in his costume, and began flirting with him, without him knowing who she was.

Testing him, she allowed him to lead her to a vacant dark bedroom, where they made love. She then left the party and returned home so that she could confront him when he returned, about his infidelity.

"Did you have a good time?" she asked sarcastically when he walked in the house.

"No, I had a lousy time," he replied. "So a few of us

left the party and went in the locker room and played poker. But the guy who borrowed my costume said he had one heck of a good time!"

I RECENTLY READ A BOOK ABOUT legends that keep reappearing in the literature as having just happened. Many gullible folks assume that anything they read in print is true, and thus believe legends like the one above have actually happened. While most of these legends are probably fiction, many are right funny.

One of my favorites is about the firemen who rescued a cat from the top of a tree. The cat's owner was very appreciative. Until as they left they backed the fire truck out of the driveway—and ran over the cat.

Another 'cat in tree' legend: A kitten was in the top of a small limber tree, and afraid to come down. Its owner had the bright idea of lassoing the top of the tree, and bending it down to where the cat could be reached. Unfortunately, just as the kitten was almost within reach, the rope broke, and the kitten went catapulting into space.

A week later they were visiting friends who lived in the neighborhood. "Let me show you our new kitten," said the host. "You won't believe this, but I was just sitting out in the yard a couple of weeks ago, when it dropped out of the sky into my lap!"

I GUESS YOU COULD ALSO CONSIDER in the category of legends, since it obviously isn't true, the story told to me by some joker in my optometric office before I retired.

"I used to have this terrible stabbing pain in my eye whenever I took my first sip of coffee", he said. "I went to a lot of specialists, and none of them could figure out why. Then I discovered it didn't happen if I took the spoon out of the cup before I took the first sip."

Another legend I love is about the state trooper who was driving through a rural Alabama area. "Pig, pig, pig!" shouted a country lady at the side of the road as he drove by.

"Redneck, redneck, redneck!" shouted the trooper at her in retaliation. As he rounded the curve in the road, he wrecked his car as he ran into a pig in the center of the road.

The Joys of Christmas Are Exaggerated?

December, 2010

All grandmothers are depicted as apple cheeked sweet little old ladies, great cooks, and a marvelous food source during the Christmas holidays. Not mine! She was a sweet lady. But she was a lousy cook.

IT'S PROBABLY BECAUSE AS I get older I become more crotchety and Scrooge-like, but it seems to me as I reflect on this past Christmas, that the joys of Christmas are often greatly exaggerated.

You may have received the Christmas card that depicts the peace and joy of going to "Grandmothers House" on Christmas Eve. The picture shows a sleigh full of smiling relatives arriving. Beautiful snow on the ground, smoke from the chimney depicting the cheery fire in the living room, a smiling Grandmother in her apron at the door, etc.

THAT ISN'T THE WAY I recall "To Grandmother's house we go" when I was a child. Instead of a peaceful sleigh, we had to travel in a nine year old Essex auto. This vehicle invariably broke down at least once during any trip. That, together with the icy roads, made the duration of the 200 mile trip from Aurora, IL to Huntington, IN a minimum of ten hours. Thus, as I remember, we arrived in a cranky mood, rather than with beaming smiles on our faces.

Granted, we were also greeted by a roaring fire in the fireplace. That's because, except for a wood stove, that was the only source of heat in the entire house. (The late newspaper columnist Leo Aikman once described his boyhood home in Indiana as also being heated only by a fire in the fireplace. "I was 21 years old before I discovered that it was possible to be warm on both sides at the same time," he once told me.)

"THE ONLY THING I COULD relate to in the joyous Grandmothers House picture, was the arrival of the sleigh full of relatives," a friend once told me. "To me they represented my Uncle Harry and his wife and bratty kids. He has lost his job again, and is arriving to move in with Grandmother and Grandfather to sponge off them for the next few months, until he sobers up and finds another job."

ANOTHER CHRISTMAS PICTORIAL representation shows a smiling family gathered around a well stocked table of delicious food, with a beautiful roasted turkey. However, my grandmother wasn't that great a cook. That, together with the main course being an old stringy chicken I had watched her catch and decapitate with an axe, didn't exactly stimulate my salivary juices. Particularly since the headless chicken had run around the yard for a few seconds before collapsing. (Honest!!)

IN ADDITION IT APPEARS to me that gift giving has often become more of an obligation, than a joyous occasion. "Everybody ought to make two lists of persons to whom he intends to send Christmas greetings," said Ed Grimsley in his book *Coming Through Awry*. "On List #1, he'd put the names of people he sincerely wanted to have a happy Christmas. On List #2 he'd put the names of people he didn't like all that much, but to whom he felt obligated ."

For example, the no-good brother-in-law with whom you've been exchanging gifts for forty years. Just because he's "family," not because you sincerely want him to have a joyous Christmas.

HOWEVER, FINDING AN APPROPRIATE gift for List #2 is less of a problem, because you needn't worry about finding something enjoyable, like you do for people on List #1. Appropriate gifts for people like the brother-in-law could include:

1. The heavy and indigestible fruitcake you've been using as a door stop since receiving it from Aunt Martha last year.
2. One of the ugly ties you receive every Christmas.
3. Della Robia mints.
4. The god-awful cheap shaving lotion, like the bottle you got last year. Its fumes somehow attract insects, but at the same time kill small birds.

IN COMPOSING THE ABOVE, I asked What's Her Name for further "bad gift" ideas. For those of you who have felt I've been picking on her in these columns, I want you to know that what goes around, comes around. The Avenger (WHN) struck, when with forked tongue she replied:

"The only other useless and undesirable gift I can think of is the book you wrote, *Fixing Stupid—Two*

Curmudgeons Pet Peeves."

And a 'bah, humbug' to her as well!

We've Lost a Bit of Sunshine

January 2011

No one ever loved a wife more than did my friend Clayton Doss. But how she put up with him, I'll never know.

WITH THE PASSING OF CLAYTON DOSS, a bit of sunshine has departed from our fair city. A clever, fun loving, always smiling, one of a kind character, he was a joy to be around.

One of the traits that made him such a character was his complete lack of organization, according to his good friend and co-worker, Billy Johnson.

"His office was always a mess. Finally when Clayton was gone, my brother Fred sent a secretary to his office to clean it up. She filled two large trash bins with trash. When Clayton returned and saw the clean office, he said, 'I can't find a durned thing in here now.' So he recovered the trash cans, took everything out of them, and put all the contents where they had been before."

And when they sold their office to Brooke Temple, Clayton decided he'd rather not move, so stayed in his same disorganized office, even after the rest of the occupants had departed. When Brooke later leased the building, he had to send someone there to move out all of Clayton's stuff, so the new tenant could move in.

WHILE NO ONE HAS EVER worshipped his wife

any more than Clayton did Betty prior to her death in 1993, he often gave her a hard time. He had a voracious appetite, and got up well over 250 pounds. So Betty put him on a strict diet. A month later she discovered that he had not lost a bit of weight. She also discovered that he had been going to Troy's every afternoon to eat four chili dogs, before going home to eat the diet food.

ANOTHER EXAMPLE OF his voracious appetite: One Friday, Betty had baked a tin of more than 30 cookies as part of the tailgate feast she was preparing for an Auburn football game the next day. That night, Clayton found he was having difficulty sleeping due to thinking about the delicious cookies in the kitchen. Finally he decided she wouldn't notice if he ate just one of them.

So into the kitchen he tiptoed. The first cookie was delicious. The second one was even better. Betty woke up the next day to discover that her tailgate menu would not include a single cookie. And he often stopped at Piggly Wiggly on the way home from work to pick up a jar of Miracle Whip and a package of cheese slices. He'd roll up a cheese slice, dip it in the Miracle Whip, and consume six or eight of them to tide him over until supper 60 minutes later.

"WE TRIED TO TEE OFF as close to noon as possible," according to Jo Stegall, who along with Ebby Brinson, belonged to Clayton's golfing group that played every Sunday afternoon. "Betty was the organist and choir director at the First Presbyterian Church, and Clayton sang in the choir. Thus he was often late to the golf course if church got out a little late. So he began leaving church early, which wasn't exactly unnoticeable to the congregation, since he left from the choir loft at the front of the church..

"'My wife told me that if I left early one more time, she was going to leave me,' he told us one Sunday while preparing to hit his first shot," said Stegall. "He teed up his ball, took a few practice swings, took his stance, and then paused and turned around to say, 'You know, I sure am gonna miss the little woman!"

HIS GOLFING COMMENTS have become legendary. Once he and his opponent were tied going into the last hole. The opponent hit a second shot that headed straight to the flag, but they could not be sure whether it cleared the trap in front of the green.

"Is my good friend in the trap, or is the sumbitch on the green?" he asked.

Another time he hit a lucky shot that caromed off an out of bounds tree, back into the fairway. "Thank you, Lord!" he said looking heavenward. Then turning to the other members of his foursome he said, "Y'all don't mind playing a fivesome, do you?"

He was so good natured that it was difficult to get his goat. Once when he was on a trip to California, some of his friends phoned him at 8:00 AM, knowing it was 5:00 AM in California. When they laughingly apologized for waking him so early, he said, "That's okay. I had to get up to answer the phone anyway."

"IF I'D KNOWN I WAS going to live this long, I'd have taken better care of myself," he often said.

I wish he had, so we'd still have him and his merriment around.

Senior Marriages Really Are Different

February 2011

At least I didn't have to get her father's permission. Plus no mother-in-law problems.

THE YOUNG MAN KEPT BRINGING girlfriends home to meet his parents. His mother found something objectionable about every one of them. Finally he found a girl exactly like his mother. But when he brought her home, his father didn't like that one.

My marriage to What's Her Name is now in its third year. During that time, I have discovered more and more differences between getting hitched later in life as opposed to early in life.

One of the advantages, as illustrated by the above story, is that in getting married when you're older you don't have any difficulties with prospective or current mothers-in-law. Other differences include:

1. Social Life: During our senior years I find that our social life consists chiefly of doctors' appointments and funerals.
2. Memory and reaction time have slowed down.

"Do you want to watch a movie tonight?" I ask

WHN.

"Let's see if anything good is on," she replies. So we go down the descriptions of each movie on ON DEMAND.

"That one looks good," she keeps saying about various ones. "Keep it in mind while we keep checking to see if there's anything better." Thirty minutes later, we can't remember which movies we thought might be good. And besides it's now too late to watch one anyway.

3. We're more set in our ways: WHN and I are very different in many ways. And of course our differences are firmly embedded over many years, and thus difficult to change. For example, she is a neat-nik and clean-nik and I am basically a slob.

Remember the story of the guy who got up in the middle of the night to go to the bathroom, and when he got back to his bed, his wife had already made it up? WHN isn't quite that bad. However one morning she had not been able to make up the bed before leaving for work, (possibly because I was still in it.) We were going out for the evening, not to return until bedtime.

"Before we go, I've got to make up the bed," she said. Since we were going to have to unmake it as soon as we got home at bedtime, the only thing I could figure was that in case we got robbed while we were gone, she was afraid the burglar would think she was a bad housekeeper.

Even though it's difficult to break old entrenched habits, nice guy that I am, I have tried to change and adapt by ceasing to be a slob. I have, for example, suggested a method for her not having to keep the house so clean in case company comes. All she has to do is arrange a number of "Get Well" cards on the mantel, so that visitors will assume she has been ill and thus unable to keep the house neat.

IN THE SPIRIT OF HELPFULNESS, I have given her other little household hints. None of which she seems to appreciate. For her edification, I read to her an article from the New York Times concerning household cleanliness, which quotes research done by University of Arizona microbiology professor Dr. Chuck Gerba:

"We found that people who had the cleanest looking kitchens were often the dirtiest. Because 'clean' people wipe up so much, they often end up spreading bacteria all over the place. The cleanest kitchens, were in the homes of bachelors, who never wiped up and just put their dirty dishes in the sink."

"In most homes," in another quote from Dr. Gerba I read to WHN, " you're better off eating off the toilet than the kitchen counter. That's partly because people tend to use antibacterial products in the bathroom but not in the kitchen."

Have I received a single word of appreciation from WHN for these tidbits of helpful advice? Not a one!!! As Rodney Dangerfield once complained, "Women! You just can't please them. My wife complained because I didn't put the toilet seat down. So I did. Now she complains about sitting on a wet toilet seat."

4. I don't hear so good: Studies have shown that women talk twice as much as men. WHN adamantly maintains that it's be-

> cause with my old-age, lousy hearing, she has to say everything twice.

Lousy hearing ain't all bad. It's a helluva lot more peaceful when you can take off your hearing aids so that you can't hear what's going on. Also beneficial in listening to some preachers.

And when I'm not in the mood for conversation at home, I can surreptitiously remove my hearing aids. Then pretend to be listening by saying, "Yes, Dear" every minute or so. In case you wish to try this technique, I must warn you that there are some dangers involved. If your wife (not mine!) asks, "Do you think my hips are getting too big?" and it happens to coincide with one of your "Yes Dears," you will be in deep doo-doo.

All in all, I have discovered that life by myself as a widower was much less complicated. But it also wasn't nearly as interesting or enjoyable!

Stress Is an Unfortunate Part of Life

August 2011

The last two articles are really not about females per se. They are advice about how to adapt to stress. And Lord knows that's what we males often need in dealing with the opposite sex.

"WHO IS IT?" SAID THE VOICE from inside the house, when the plumber knocked at the door.

"It's the plumber," he called out, not realizing it was a parrot to whom he was responding.

"Who is it?" said the parrot again. Actually, those were the only three words he could speak, so responded to everything that way.

"It's the plumber," he replied, more loudly this time.

"Who is it?" said the parrot.

"IT'S THE PLUMBER, it's the plumber!" he screamed at the top of his voice. He then became so stressed by his frustration, he fell over dead from a heart attack.

A few minutes later, the couple returned home, and discovered the body on their doorstep. As the husband turned the body over, his wife asked, "Who is it?"

"It's the plumber!" shouted the parrot.

STRESS IS, UNFORTUNATELY A PART of life we have to put up with. However, over the years I've learned there are ways to help reduce it. One of them that has been helpful to me came from a cardiologist who said, "There are only two rules of life. #1. Don't sweat the small stuff. #2. It's all small stuff."

The plumber is a good example of what can happen if we get all worked up over unimportant things, or things over which we have little or no control.

ANOTHER RULE I LEARNED I've found helpful, is to wherever possible eliminate the source of the stress. Forty years ago, I had never learned to say no to various church and civic volunteer job requests, and consequently was doing a whole lot of things I really hated because I thought it was my civic duty. And ended up having a stroke while still in my 40's.

Old timers may remember Dr. Ed Gates, who was a neurologist here in Rome. "I moved here from Detroit," he once told me, "to get away from the stress of practicing in a big city."

"You have to eliminate all the sources of stress you can," he told me, when he examined me following the stroke. "When I was practicing in Detroit, I found that most of the men having strokes and heart attacks while still in their 40's, were the junior executives at the automobile plants, who were under constant stress. Wherever possible, you need to reduce stress by doing only the things you enjoy doing."

So I learned to say no to many of the volunteer jobs, found my life much easier, and am still alive and kicking 40 years later.

UNFORTUNATELY, AS WITH THE AUTO executives, it's not always possible to cease doing things you don't like. For example: "I'm not going to school today!" he pouted. "All of the kids hate me, and so do the teachers."

"But you can't just decide not to go," replied his mother.

"Why not?"

"Because you're 42 years old, and principal of the school, that's why not."

ONE THING I TEND TO FORGET it is that we do need to have *some* stress, in order to keep life interesting. When I graduated from high school, I spent the summer working in a factory, to earn money for college expenses. I was assigned to help a gentleman who had been working on the same job for over 25 years. Day after day, all day long, he did the same routine job of every few seconds, placing metal sheets in a stamping machine, ad infinitum.

"They offered me a job as foreman a long time ago, but I didn't want all that hassle." He told me. He had eliminated all stress in his job, and replaced it with utter boredom.

BUT IT WOULD BE NICE not to have too much stress like the small business owner I heard about:

"Why are you so stressed?" someone asked him.

"We're looking for a treasurer," he replied.

"But I thought you just hired a new treasurer a few months ago."

"We did. That's the one we're looking for!"

Some Guaranteed Ways to Relieve Stress

October 2011

Handling the stress of living with women is too big a topic to be covered in just one article. Hence here is part 2.

"MA'AM, IT'S AGAINST THE LAW to drive just 20 miles an hour on an interstate," said the state trooper after stopping an elderly lady driver.

"But the sign says the speed limit is 20," she protested.

"No ma'am, that's the route number. You're driving on Route 20. And by the way, why do the other three ladies in your car appear to be so stressed?"

"I don't know. Unless it's because we just came off of Route 119."

You may recall that last month's column was about overcoming stress. I ran out of space before I ran out of words. Thus this is a continuation of the same theme.

"LIFE CONSISTS NOT OF WHAT happens to you, but instead how you react." Thus wrote some wise philosopher, whose name escapes me.

"Things turn out best for people who make the best of the way things turn out," is the way Art Linkletter put it.

An example is a story told about Muhammed Ali when he was heavyweight boxing champion. He was on a plane, and the stewardess asked him to fasten his seat belt.

"Superman don't need no seat belt!" he said, and refused to fasten it. The stewardess could have started an argument, and become angry and stressed about his refusal. Instead she replied, "That's right. And Superman don't need no airplane either."

ANOTHER EXAMPLE I LIKE about not getting upset about stressful things I read in the *Rome News-Tribune,* quoting Loran Smith when he spoke at Darlington recently. He told of pumping gas at a service station, when an elderly gentleman in an old pick up truck drove up to the next pump. Making conversation with him, Smith said, "The price of gas sure is awful isn't it?"

"Don't bother me none," said the gent. "I always get just ten dollars worth anyway, no matter what they're chargin'."

"NOTHING ERASES UNPLEASANT thoughts more effectively than concentration on pleasant ones," said noted stress researcher Hans Selye. Or as some comic once said, "Humor in stress situations is like a diaper. It doesn't change things permanently, but makes everything better for awhile!"

THE SUPPORT OF YOUR FAMILY can also help you reduce any stress you're going through. "Your husband has had a heart attack due to stress," said the MD. "For him to recover, you're going to have to take good care of him.

"You can't nag him, you must submit to every request he makes, stay home with him 24 hours a day, watch TV football with him, fix him three good meals every day, make love with him every night if he wishes, and do exactly whatever he asks. Otherwise he's going to die."

"What did the doctor say?" her husband anxiously inquired.

"He said, 'You're gonna die!" she replied.

I DON'T KNOW THAT I WOULD recommend the following way of eliminating stress, even though it worked for this lady:

"Any history of eye disease in your family?" I once asked a patient during case history when I was still practicing optometry.

"Yes, my grandmother has glaucoma," he said.

"Is she undergoing any treatment for it?"

"She read someplace that marijuana could help lower the pressure, so she's smoking pot for it," he said.

"Is it helping any?" I asked.

"Yes, and no. She can't see any better, but now she don't give a damn."

YOU ALSO NEED FRIENDS to help support you in times of stress. So you'd better make sure you have some. Don't be like:

"Why don't you play golf with George anymore?" the wife asked her husband.

"Would you play golf with someone who cheats, moves his ball when you're not looking, and lies about his score?" he asked.

"Well, no, I guess not," she replied.

"Neither will George!"

I'LL LEAVE YOU WITH ONE more stupid story about stress relief. It's about the gentleman who decided he would help eliminate stress by quitting work and doing extensive traveling. Also that he would place a thumb tack on a world map on each country he visited.

He realized his first two destinations had to be the

countries on the top right and top left of the map. Otherwise the map would fall off the wall.

About the Author

JACK RUNNINGER WAS BORN in 1923 in Aurora, Illinois. His college education at DePauw U. was interrupted by Naval service during World War II, including participation in the invasions of Iwo Jima and Okinawa. After the war he married high school sweetheart Mary Gibson, just in time for her to work his way through Optometry School. After graduation he practiced optometry for more than 40 years in Rome, GA.

In addition to practicing optometry, he wrote a monthly humor column for national optometric journals for some 30 years. None of his fellow eye doctors ever accused him of being the most brilliant eye doctor in practice, but many did accuse him of being the funniest.

"MARK TWAIN AND WILL ROGERS left this world before Runninger's readers even came into it, and that is reason enough for us to enjoy those funny events he describes in his columns." said Bob Koetting, O.D., leading contact lens practitioner and guru.

"Jack Runninger is the Mark Twain, the Art Buchwald, and the Dave Barry of the eyeball world," according to Ben Milder, M.D., ophthalmologist and award winning author.

His humor even made its way overseas. "The Jack Runninger column has always been a must-read for me, particularly for the wry smile his humour (Australian spelling of the word) provokes," said Damien

Smith, AM, DOS, PhD, Australia, President of the World Council of Optometry.

DURING HIS CAREER HE did fool enough folks to be able to garner a few honors: National Optometry Hall of Fame; Honorary Doctor of Ocular Science from his alma mater; Lifetime Achievement Award, also from his alma mater; and "Distinguished Practitioner and Member, National Academies of Practice."

Springing from the success of his optometric columns, he began writing humor columns for his local newspaper, the Rome, (GA), *News-Tribune,* from whence cometh the articles in this book. They have received state and national awards.

AFTER FIRST WIFE MARY passed away in 2006, two years later he married a lovely widow, Helen Hayes Cobb, (referred to as "What's Her Name" or WHN in these pages). She was executive director of a center for mentally challenged adults, which according to a number of his wiseass friends, made her ideal for him. Fortunately both wives were good sports about the rash things he had to say about them.

"My plan is to live forever," he says. "So far so good."

His email address is runningerj@comcast.net. If you wish to order a copy of this book, send your mailing address and a check for $17.45 (includes $2.50 shipping) to:

Jack Runninger
2663 N. Broad Ext.
Rome, GA, 30161

CPSIA information can be obtained at www.ICGtesting.com
Printed in the USA
LVOW080626030212

266880LV00001B/3/P